The World Is Charged:

Poetic Engagements with Gerard Manley Hopkins

For Stephen Gardner and John Wood

THE WORLD IS CHARGED:

POETIC ENGAGEMENTS WITH GERARD MANLEY HOPKINS

ൠ

Edited by

DANIEL WESTOVER AND WILLIAM WRIGHT

With an Afterword by

PAUL MARIANI

CLEMSON UNIVERSITY PRESS

Works produced at Clemson University by the Center for Electronic and Digital Publishing (CEDP), including *The South Carolina Review* and its themed series "Virginia Woolf International," "Ireland in the Arts and Humanities," and "James Dickey Revisited," may be found at our website: http://www.clemson.edu/cedp/press. Contact the director at 864-656-5399 for information.

ISBN 978-1-942954-20-0

Published by Clemson University Press at the Center for Electronic and Digital Publishing, Clemson University, Clemson, South Carolina.

Produced with Adobe Creative Cloud software and Microsoft Word. This book is set in Adobe Garamond Pro and was printed and bound by CPI Group (UK) Ltd, Croydon, CR0 4YY

Editorial Assistants: Sam Martin, Charis Chapman

Cover design by Chad Pelton.

Contents

Acknowledgments

Daniel Westover

I'd like to thank my wife, Mary, and my daughters, Eden and Branwen, for supporting and inspiring my work. Their care and encouragement make projects like this one possible. I would also like to thank my dear friends John and Carol Wood, whose love of Hopkins stirred my interest in his work many years ago.

Thanks are also due to Fr. Brian McClorry, S.J., for his hospitality while I stayed at St. Beuno's "on a pastoral forehead of Wales" and conducted research relating to Hopkins and the work he wrote while living there.

I'm deeply grateful to the College of Arts and Sciences and the Office of Research and Sponsored Programs at East Tennessee State University for a generous travel award that allowed me to launch this book at the 2016 Gerard Manley Hopkins International Literary Festival at Newbridge College, Co. Kildare, Ireland.

Finally, I'd like to thank William Wright for embarking on this project with me and for seeing it through with diligence, zeal, and humor.

William Wright

I'd like to thank my wife, Michelle, who encouraged me during this project and whose patience and support helped make this book a reality. I thank Joseph Feeney, S.J. and Paul Mariani, whose enthusiasm emboldened Dan and me to make this book.

Last and certainly *not* least, I thank Daniel Westover, whose kindness, assiduity, and workflow proved aspirational for me and have been an absolute necessity for this collection. He has been a wonderful collaborator.

෨

We both wish to thank John Morgenstern, Managing Editor at Clemson University Press, Wayne Chapman, Director of Clemson University Press, and Anthony Cond, Managing Director of Liverpool University Press for their belief in this project and for the time and careful attention they have devoted to it.

Our deepest appreciation and gratitude are for the poets included in this anthology for their excitement, generosity, and patience.

෨

We are grateful to the authors and publishers of the books below for permission to reprint poems in this anthology:

Allen Braden: "Taboo against the Word *Beauty*, Ornithological Version on Aesthetic Theory" is reprinted from *A Wreath of Down and Drops of Blood* (University of Georgia Press, 2010).
Robin Chapman: "Dappled Things," "Fire," "Landscape," and "Spare" are reprinted from *Dappled Things* (Revue K, 2013).
Carolyn Creedon: "Pied Beauty" is reprinted from *Wet* (Kent State University Press, 2012).

Philip Dacey: "A Dream of Hopkins," "A Simple Garden Ladder," and "The Sleep" are reprinted from *Gerard Manley Hopkins Meets Walt Whitman in Heaven and Other Poems* (Penmaen Press, 1982).
Meg Day: "Aubade for One Still Uncertain of Being Born" is reprinted from *Last Psalm at Sea Level* (Barrow Street Press, 2014).
Desmond Egan: "Hopkins in Kildare" is reprinted from *Hopkins in Kildare* (Goldsmith Press, 2012).
Jesse Graves: "Goldengrove" is reprinted from *Basin Ghosts* (Texas Review Press, 2014).
Eve Grubin: "Date" is reprinted from *Morning Prayer* (Sheep Meadow Press, 2006).
Jane Hicks: "My Second-Grade Teacher Reads Us Gerard Manley Hopkins" is reprinted from *Driving with the Dead* (University Press of Kentucky, 2014).
Kimberly Johnson: "Pater Noster" ("The garden is a miracle.") and "Spring Again" are reprinted from *Leviathan with a Hook*. Copyright © 2002 by Kimberley Johnson. "A Psalm of Ascents" is reprinted from *A Metaphorical God*. Copyright © 2008 by Kimberley Johnson. All reprinted with the permission of Persea Books, Inc. (New York), www.perseabooks.com.
Gwyneth Lewis: "The Telegraph Baby" and "Red Kites at Tregaron" are reprinted from *Chaotic Angels* (Bloodaxe Books, 2005).
Amit Majmudar: "Instructions to an Artisan" is reprinted from *0°, 0°: Poems*. Copyright © 2009 by Amit Majmudar. Published 2009 by TriQuarterly Books/Northwestern University Press. All rights reserved. "Prayer" and "The Christ-Frost" are reprinted from *Heaven and Earth*. Copyright © 2011 by Amit Majmudar. Published 2011 by Story Line Press. Used by permission of Story Line Press, an imprint of Red Hen Press. "Horse Apocalypse" is reprinted from *Dothead: Poems* by Amit Majmudar, copyright © 2016 by Amit Majmudar. Used by permission of Alfred A. Knopf, an imprint of Knopf Doubleday Publishing Group, a division of Penguin Random House LLC. All rights reserved.
Sandra Marchetti: "Migration Theory" and "Never-Ending Birds" are reprinted from *Confluence* (Sundress Publications, 2015).
Susan Laughter Meyers: "Coastland" is reprinted from *My Dear, Dear Stagger Grass* (Cider Press Review, 2013).
Robert Morgan: "Algae," "Aspen Song," "Left Behind," and "Maple Gall" are reprinted from *Dark Energy* by Robert Morgan, copyright © 2015 by Robert Morgan. Used by permission of Penguin Books, an imprint of Penguin Publishing Group, a division of Random House LLC.
Melissa Range: "The Canary," "Christ Imagined as Calvary Commander," "October Trees," and "Prayer to the Birds" are reprinted from *Horse and Rider* (Texas Tech University Press, 2010).
Ron Rash: "The Corpse Bird" is reprinted from *Among the Believers* (Iris Press, 2000). "Speckled Trout" and "Fall Creek" are reprinted from *Raising the Dead* (Iris Press, 2002). "Dylan Thomas" is reprinted from *Waking* (Hub City Press, 2014).
Don Share: "Savior" is reprinted from *Union* (Eyewear Publishing, 2013).
Mary Szybist: "Via Negativa" and "In Tennessee I Found a Firefly" are reprinted from *Granted*. Copyright © 2003 by Mary Szybist. Reprinted with the permission of The Permissions Company, Inc., on behalf of Alice James Books, www.alicejames.org. "Knocking or Nothing" is reprinted from *Incarnadine*. Copyright © 2012 by Mary Szybist. Reprinted with the permission of The Permissions Company, Inc., on behalf of Graywolf Press, Minneapolis, Minnesota, www.graywolfpress.org.
R. K. R. Thornton: "Gerard Manley Hopkins (1884–1889)" is reprinted from *Adlestrophes* (Rectory Press, 2014).
John Wood: "Η Ποιητική" is reprinted from *The Gates of the Elect Kingdom* (University of Iowa Press, 1997); "A Sestina for Mishima" is reprinted from *The Fictions of History* (21st Editions, 2011).
Charles Wright: "Jesuit Graves" is reprinted from *Black Zodiac*. Copyright © 1997 by Charles Wright. Reprinted by permission of Farrar Straus and Giroux, LLC. "There Is a Balm in Gilead" is reprinted from *Buffalo Yoga*. Copyright © 2004 by Charles Wright. Reprinted by permission of Farrar Straus and Giroux, LLC.
Willliam Wright: "Aubade for Yellow Jacket" and "A Path through Walnut Trees after Rain" are reprinted from *Tree Heresies* (Mercer University Press, 2015).

Foreword

℘

"It strikes like lightnings to hear him sing": A first encounter with Gerard Manley Hopkins and the Genesis of this Anthology

Stephen Gardner, my undergraduate poetry mentor, introduced me to Gerard Manley Hopkins by way of a British poetry course offered at the University of South Carolina Aiken in 1998. I was nineteen, idealistic, poetry-crazed, and heartbroken: my parents had just divorced, and I was not taking it well. I associate that time with an image as much Eliotic as Hopkinsian: a great cathedral stained-glass window pulled from its sashes to explode into unassimilable, gemlike shards—a barbarous beauty, but beauty nonetheless. Stephen was not religious, but he always mentioned Hopkins in his classes, even during an American survey course in which he argued that Hopkins outpaced Whitman and Dickinson in terms of raw power and genius—a provocative claim, but one he supported for the rest of the class with fervent certainty.

Stephen delighted in reading Hopkins aloud, and I distinctly recall the way his voice thrummed through the air of that tiny classroom as he read "God's Grandeur." In my mind, Stephen remains unmatched for his ability to read poetry with a convincing dynamism, and on that day, after the brown brink had sprung in the east and the Holy Ghost had wrapped its protective, luminous wings around the imminent hatching of Earth's nature, Stephen shivered and said, "It gives me chills every single time."

The poem struck me with a nearly hallucinogenic force. Not only did I experience a physiological reaction, one in which the electricity of the poem seemed to permeate me deeply and rush me with nature's "dearest freshness," but the poem's stark and unharnessed lyrical beauty also provoked an emotional response too difficult to be contained in that stifling room: I rose, exited the building, walked to my car, got in, and wept. "God's Grandeur" was more than anodyne to my sadness; it struck me as a general hope for the understanding and acknowledgment of beauty in the world, no matter the "blear," "smear," and "toil" of humanity's problems, personal or otherwise. It was one of a handful of truly epiphanic moments in my life thus far. "God's Grandeur" became the first poem I memorized, followed by "The Windhover" and "Pied Beauty." The more I read Hopkins, the more I delighted in the kaleidoscopic images and lush sounds, and the more firmly Hopkins linked with my understanding of poetry. What he writes in "Spring" well describes my response: "it strikes like lightnings to hear him sing."

My first, forceful response notwithstanding, Hopkins's poetry has only grown increasingly more powerful and complex over time, with the passionate, often frenzied currents of his words seeming to amplify as I age. His combinations of sounds and senses lead to new wisdoms that I simply do not find in other poets. Thus, my own poems are, and likely will forever be, influenced by my love for Hopkins, and the power and idiosyncrasy of his poetry has helped shape the contours of my preference for, and preoccupation with, sonic texture and lyrical passion in contemporary poetry.

In this esteem for Gerard Manley Hopkins I am hardly alone. Indeed, Daniel Westover, my co-editor, and I knew that numerous Anglophone poets of the twentieth century drew inspiration from Hopkins. Many of these poets are explored in Dan's introduction and Paul Mariani's afterword (I would like to add to that coterie James Dickey, whose poetry from the late fifties into the early seventies radiates with an incantatory power derived at least in part from Hopkins). It was evident to us that much contemporary poetry continues to claim a Hopkinsian influence. As we corresponded about this, sharing ideas and new poetic discoveries, we eventually concluded that the extent of Hopkins's impact on contemporary poetry warranted, indeed *necessitated*, a volume of Hopkins-inspired poetry, if for no other reason than to bring an awareness of his far-reaching influence to a wider audience. Dan and I decided to center the volume on living poets—and also to include many younger ones—not merely as a practicality, but primarily to demonstrate the ongoing reach of Hopkins's influence. We are proud to provide an edition in which many well-known poets—including Charles Wright, who agreed to be part of this project while serving as U.S. Poet Laureate—are published alongside gifted younger writers like Melissa Range and Steven Collier Brown.

Whether through subtleties of sound or diction, likeminded aesthetic philosophy, thematic similarities, or even a proclivity for pastiche, these contemporary poems "rinse and ring the ear," charged with the life of Hopkins's indefatigable legacy. They bear witness that his strangeness, his celebration of dappled things and their unifying distinctions, thrives in the minds of many of today's best writers. Dan and I anticipate that Hopkins's influence will continue to take root, and that it will blossom in the words of many future poets.

William Wright

Introduction

"Counter, Original, Spare, Strange": Gerard Manley Hopkins and Contemporary Poetry

strange /streɪn(d)ʒ/ *10. Unfamiliar, abnormal, or exceptional to a degree that excites wonder or astonishment; difficult to take in or account for; queer, surprising, unaccountable. (OED)*

There is, I have noted in my teaching, a certain emotional energy students bring to class after their first encounter with Gerard Manley Hopkins. Part bewilderment, part whiplash, it is also, always, *awe*. Their usual method—treating poems like puzzles to decipher—has yielded no fruit. They have encountered too much compression and coinage, too many shifts in syntax to pin down a paraphrase. Where they have previously come to class with carefully prepared summaries, they now find that they cannot separate what Hopkins is saying (insofar as they can discern it) from the manner of its saying. Instead, they return talking about language: layered metaphor, idiosyncratic diction, wrenching syntax, patterned assonance, and alliterative flurries. In other words, they want (at last!) to talk about poetry, and this, ironically, because poetry—indeed language itself—has been defamiliarized, in the Shklovskian sense of something *made strange*.

For Hopkins, to be strange is to praise and perform creation. It is to quicken, to cry out and, yes, to dislocate at times in an unswerving attempt to strike wonder. In his poems, each part of nature speaks God's peculiar vocabulary; each word-jolt or jarring phrase points to the maker of "all things counter, original, spare, strange."[1] Language in Hopkins is sacramental because the word is more than signifier—it is *incarnation*. He once wrote, "The world then is word, expression, news of God."[2] For all his verbal dynamism, Hopkins did not believe in strangeness for its own sake, and he disliked other nineteenth-century poets (most notably Swinburne) who, in his view, used poetic devices as vainglorious adornment. One of many Hopkinsian paradoxes is that this most distinctive of poets does not view language as an extension of the ego. Instead, he reveres each word's *inscape*—his term for distinctive, exercised identity—a Romantic idea derived in part from the aesthetic philosophy of his Oxford mentor Walter Pater and in part from Duns Scotus's idea of *haecceitas,* or "thisness." Even in first-person poems, the speaker never usurps the individuality of things. For example, in his most famous sonnet, "The Windhover," Hopkins begins with himself—"I caught this morning morning's minion" (1)—but quickly recedes, giving precedence to "the achieve of; the mastery of *the thing*" (8, italics mine). In the work of some lyric poets, all nature is appropriated, subsumed into the speaker's song of self. In the poems of Gerard Manley Hopkins, each part of the world "*selves—goes itself*"[3] and in so doing becomes a distinct part of the body of Christ.

Hopkins, then, presents the spare and strange—the unique—as part of a spiritual whole. In Coleridgean terms, a Gerard Manley Hopkins poem is "unity in multeity."[4] Because he abjured apathy, Hopkins sought language that might shock and astonish.

Perhaps more than any other poet, he was obsessed with words and their infinitely variable, infinitely peculiar combinations. His journals contain lists of words connected by etymology, by sound, or by idiosyncratic association: "Crook, crank, kranke, crick, cranky…."[5] Sometimes these read like wonderful tongue twisters: "*Slip, slipper, slop, slabby* (muddy), *slide*, perhaps *slope*, but if *slope* is thus connected what are we to say of *slant*?"[6] Word lists are everywhere in the poems, too: "Earnest, earthless, equal, attuneable, vaulty, voluminous…";[7] "swift, slow; sweet, sour, adazzle, dim…."[8] Hopkins makes us see the *thingness* of words; he renders them strange, displays them as unique objects even as he combines them. As a result, his language refuses any illusion of being transparent. Rather, it asserts its tactility and musicality. In his correspondence with Robert Bridges, Hopkins repeatedly emphasized aurality, insisting that his "verse is less to be read than heard….it is oratorical."[9] When Bridges's friend Andrew Lang dismissed the poems as willfully odd, Hopkins countered, "Take breath and read it with the ears, as I always wish to be read, and my verse becomes all right."[10] Elsewhere, he maintained that even his most "strange constructions would be dramatic and effective" when read aloud.[11]

In order to make language dramatic, Hopkins unsettles it; he breaks, combines, inverts, and compresses it, re-purposing phonemes and phrases like a re-mix artist, an S.J. DJ. Instead of "Stones ring and tumble down round wells," he writes that "tumbled over rim in roundy wells / Stones ring," making "tumbled over…wells" a modifier. After the line break, the initial spondee truly rings out, having been set up by the alliteration, assonance, rolling rhythm, and disorientating grammar of the previous line.[12] Hopkins's reverence for language does not equate to his leaving it alone. On the contrary, he mixes and blends existing words like paint on a palette to create new, shockingly vivid colors of diction. In fact, it was partly Hopkins's training as a visual artist that led to the creation of his innovative soundscapes. He sketched regularly until 1875, the year he broke a long poetic silence and began work on "The Wreck of the *Deutschland*," at which time he stopped drawing and rededicated his imagistic power to poetry. He felt like God had "touch[ed] [him] afresh,"[13] and his zeal is evident in the poems. In "The Windhover," for example, Hopkins describes a heart stirred from its hiding place, and he proceeds to unleash a blizzard of euphoric diction. The poem praises the valorous Christ-falcon, certainly, but it also celebrates a poet's resurrection into words. And it is with words that any discussion of Hopkins should begin and end. In the introduction to his *Oxford Book of Modern Verse* (1936), W. B. Yeats calls Hopkins's oeuvre "a last development of poetic diction," and he describes the meaning of a Hopkins poem as something that "comes out of words, passes to and fro between them, and goes back into words."[14] More than a fitting assessment of Hopkins's work, this is as good a description of modern lyric poetry as one is likely to find.

Another reason Hopkins's poetry rings strange to the English ear is that it reverberates with Welsh tones. While his debt to classical and Anglo-Saxon verse forms is well known (he mentions Greek and Latin lyrics, as well as *Piers Plowman*, in his preface to the poems), his response to Welsh-language poetry is underappreciated. Hopkins spent three of his happiest years (1874–1877) at St. Beuno's, a Jesuit theological college overlooking the Vale of Clwyd in North Wales, and it was here, while he was learning the Welsh language, that he composed many of his best-known poems, including "The Wreck of the *Deutschland*," "The Windhover," "God's Grandeur," "Pied Beauty," "The Starlight Night,"

"Spring" and "As kingfishers catch fire"—all poems of praise and elegy, the prevailing modes within the Welsh tradition. Indeed, beginning with "The Wreck of the *Deutschland*," Hopkins's poems incorporate elements of Welsh *cynghanedd* ("chiming"), which he read and even composed. While he loosens the strict rules that have governed *cynghanedd* since the fourteenth century, he draws pervasively upon its alliterative patterns. Consider, as one example, the line "Of the Yore-flood, of the year's fall" (250) from "The Wreck of the *Deutschland*." This is an adaptation of *cynghanedd groes*, or cross harmony. Like Anglo-Saxon verse, *cynghanedd* uses a divided line, but where Anglo-Saxon verse requires only the stressed consonants in the first half to appear in the second, *cynghanedd groes* ups the ante, requiring all consonants to repeat and to repeat in the same order, as they do here. The poem "The Sea and the Skylark" is also Welsh-inspired, but in this instance Hopkins is less faithful to consonant order, instead electing to amp up the frequency of his "chiming" as he adapts Welsh patterns to an English line:

> Left hand, off land, I hear the lark ascend,
>   His rash-fresh re-winded new-skeinèd score
>   In crisps of curl off wild winch whirl, and pour
> And pelt music, till none's to spill nor spend.

This is an iambic pentameter, *ABBA* quatrain, but liberal substitutions disguise this, as does chiming within and across lines. In addition to the obvious repetition of initial consonants, the first two lines also contain five instances of "vowel + nd" combinations—*hand, land, ascend, winded, skeinèd*—and these create both consonant chiming and internal rhyme, a kind of dragging *(lusg)* of consonants that is characteristic of *cynghanedd*. The same sounds that begin some words end others, and the level of assonance is such that one hardly notices there is end rhyme at all. Scanned, this is a modified *ABBA* English quatrain, but in practice, the poem's architecture is constructed with Welsh-derived, intra-woven sound repetition much more than with meter, and the result is a poem with a strangely un-English sound. Like so many other Hopkins poems, "The Sea and the Skylark" was written in what Hopkins called "My Welsh days…when I was fascinated with *cynghanedd*."[15] On another occasion, he wrote, "The chiming of consonants I got in part from the Welsh, which is very rich in sound and imagery."[16] These innovations are key features of Hopkins's "sprung rhythm," the theory of which he first articulated at St. Beuno's.[17]

We see, then, that to be strange in the Hopkinsian sense is to bend and defy categories, and this is also true of his place in literary history. Many of his concerns—industrialism, religious faith and doubt, science, language—were common among Victorian writers, and in this sense Hopkins is clearly a poet of his age, but in his style he differs radically from his contemporaries. Because he writes experimental verse, he has often been regarded as a proto-modernist, more at home in the twentieth century than in his own, but this placement is likewise problematic. It is true that his vigorous stress patterns were well received in a post-WWI literary landscape (*Poems of Gerard Manley Hopkins* was first published a month after the armistice), and his dark sonnets now seem prophetic in their grappling for meaning in the midst of trauma. But Hopkins avoids the self-conscious allusiveness and indirectness that typify high modernist poetry. Unlike T. S. Eliot, for example, whose work is always a conscious conversation with the past, Hopkins insists upon the performing present. And unlike the imagists, who insisted on the language and rhythms of common speech, Hopkins, while he prefigures the imagists in his verbal precision and immediacy, nevertheless extols peculiar phrasings, rare rhythms, singular sounds. Where many twentieth-century poets break down the self and question the efficacy of direct speech by throwing their voices (and their emotions) upon objective correlatives, Hopkins eschews ventriloquism. He insists, rather, on the emotive vitality and authenticity of every thing and the power of language to embody identity. Even his "Terrible Sonnets"—heart-wrenching poems of anguish and submission—venerate "thisness." In these poems, the speaker must worship God *via negativa*, but his words—which for Hopkins are the Word incarnate—bear witness of God *via positiva*. In this way Hopkins stands aside from most high modernist poetry. Eliot knew this, arguing that "Hopkins…is not so much a poet of our time as the accidents of his publication and the inventions of his metrics have led us to suppose."[18]

It is partly because Hopkins cannot be pigeonholed that he has, in terms of influence, remained relevant for almost a century. In his strange creations, poets of multiple generations have found an openness of feeling, rhythmic freshness, and relish for sound that is often lacking among their contemporaries. Some of the foremost poets of the twentieth century—Ivor Gurney, W. H. Auden, Dylan Thomas, Robert Lowell, John Berryman, Robert Hayden, Elizabeth Bishop, Sylvia Plath, Seamus Heaney, Randall Jarrell, and Geoffrey Hill—have counted Hopkins as a foundational influence, and through their work as well as his own, Hopkins has entered the mainstream of contemporary poetry. Bishop, for example, frequently mentions Hopkins in letters and interviews, admiring his power of perception and what she called his "poetic psychology," which she defined as "the mind in action rather than repose."[19] Plath, too, often mentions Hopkins in her journals, looking to him as a source of healing: "…all the despair, coming at me when I am most weak. I will read Hopkins: and, when our lives crack, and the loveliest mirror cracks, is it not right to rest, to step aside and heal[?]"[20] On another occasion, she made this brief but powerful entry: "Meanwhile, read Hopkins for solace."[21] Plath also responded to Hopkins's style. Her early poem "Ode to Ted" (1956), written for Ted Hughes, is as Hopkinsian as anything in this anthology:

> For his least look, scant eyes yield:
> each finger-furrowed field
> heaves forth stalk, leaf, fruit-nubbed emerald;
> bright grain sprung so rarely
> he hauls to his will early;
> at his hand's staunch hest, birds build.[22]

The aggressive alliteration, stress clusters, compound adjectives, and uncommon syntax obviously recall Hopkins, and when Plath refers to the grain as "sprung," she winks at Hughes, acknowledging her source. Similarly, "heaves forth" echoes "fathers-forth" from "Pied Beauty." Plath's later work is less obviously derivative of Hopkins, but his influence is still apparent. Heaney also imbibed and imitated Hopkins early on. In fact, he named Hopkins as the reason he began writing poems at all, describing the impact in physical terms: "It was a matter of sensation, little ricochets and chain reactions within the nervous system…like getting verbal gooseflesh. And, naturally enough, when I wrote my first poems…I wrote in Hopkins-speak."[23] The Nobel laureate-to-be would soon find his own way of speaking, but Hopkins's influence is evident even in Heaney's mature poetry. In terms of style, thematic choices, and critical reception, Elizabeth Bishop, Sylvia Plath, and Seamus Heaney could hardly be more different. Yet their shared admiration for Gerard Manley Hopkins is a common denominator.

And so it is with the poets in this anthology, dissimilar in many ways but comparable in their esteem for Hopkins's strange genius. Our title, *The World Is Charged: Poetic Engagements with Gerard Manley Hopkins*, suggests both a wide-ranging influence and a diversity of poetic responses. In these pages, readers will encounter poetry that alludes to Hopkins's life or to specific Hopkins poems, poetry that shares his aesthetic or spiritual philosophy, and poetry that adopts or adapts his patterns of stress and sound. Some poems are overt in their debt while others are understated, but each validates our premise, namely that Gerard Manley Hopkins (however we place him historically) is one of the most important forerunners of contemporary poetry. His influence is manifest in Amit Majmudar's chiming lines yoked to spiritual themes, in Kimberly Johnson's prayerful yearning, in Melissa Range's woven sound structures, in Joan Houlihan's alliterative virtuosity, and in Ron Rash's Welsh-inspired forms. His echoes resonate in Robin Chapman's hypnotic diction, in Cheryl Stiles's playful syntax, in Derek Sheffield's verbal precision, and in Robert Morgan's reverence for the inscape of every object. Indeed, this book proves that Hopkins's influence is enabling to poets from diverse backgrounds and at many different stages of their development, just as stimulating, for example, to Georgia Edwards—a writer who, in her sixties, is publishing her first poem in this anthology—as he is to Charles Wright, who recently finished his tenure as Poet Laureate of the United States. As in the work of Hopkins, the strange genius of these writers is best appreciated when their poems are read aloud, with an ear—indeed with a whole body—tuned to the ways in which their sound and conceptual patterns work together. The poems, of course, are distinct utterances, separate strings; "each…finds tongue to fling out broad its name."[24] Yet in the context of this volume, they also speak to each other, and together, in stirring ways, not only echoing their shared poetic predecessor, but also asserting his continuing significance in our contemporary world.

By bringing these voices together, William Wright and I are suggesting an alternative poetic narrative. In Hopkinsian terms, this book is *counter*. In a climate where high modernism is often held up as contemporary poetry's predominant forerunner, we propose a more complex genealogy, tracing back to Hopkins and his influential early admirers current strands of emotional and spiritual openness, pleasure in word play and sonic textures, and veneration of the dynamic material world. We see the 1918 publication of *Poems of Gerard Manley Hopkins* as a vital touchstone, a kind of lightning rod moment that shaped the direction of modern literature and that continues to impact new generations of writers. *The World Is Charged: Poetic Engagements with Gerard Manley Hopkins* is the first of two volumes devoted to beginning an important conversation, one that explores Hopkins's wide-ranging and continuing influence. The second volume, *The Fire that Breaks: Gerard Manley Hopkins's Poetic Legacies*, will be a collection of critical essays examining various manifestations of Hopkins's influence throughout the twentieth century and leading up to the present moment—a moment represented by the current anthology. Both books will be useful to scholars looking for new ways of approaching contemporary verse via poetic antecedents. The present anthology will be especially helpful for teachers of contemporary poetry and for teachers of Hopkins's work, who might share the poems with students as a way of bringing Hopkins to a new audience and demonstrating his enduring influence. To all of our readers, whether poets, teachers, critics, scholars, or bibliophiles, we offer this work as witness: the strange influence of Gerard Manley Hopkins is a freshness deep down things, and (so far at least) it is never spent.

Daniel Westover

Notes

1. "Pied Beauty," line 7.

2. From Hopkins's notes, Aug. 7, 1882. Qtd. in Christopher Devlin, S.J. (ed.), *The Sermons and Devotional Writings of Gerard Manley Hopkins* (London: OUP, 1959), p. 129.

3. "As kingfishers catch fire, dragonflies draw flame," line 7. Italics mine.

4. Samuel Taylor Coleridge, "On Poesy or Art," *Biographia Literaria*, qtd. in Timothy Corrigan, *Coleridge, Language and Criticism* (Athens, GA: U of Georgia P, 1982), p. 152.

5. Qtd. in Cary H. Plotkin, *The Tenth Muse: Victorian Philology and the Genesis of the Poetic Language of Gerard Manley Hopkins* (Carbondale, IL: Southern Illinois UP, 1989), p. 102.

6. Qtd. in Garrett Stewart, *Reading Voices: Literature and the Phonotext* (Berkeley: U of California P, 1990). p. 176.

7. "Spelt from Sibyl's Leaves," line 1.

8. "Pied Beauty," line 9.

9. Letter to Robert Bridges, Aug. 21, 1877. *The Letters of Gerard Manley Hopkins to Robert Bridges*, ed. C. C. Abbott (London: Oxford UP, 1955), p. 46.

10. Letter to Robert Bridges, Apr. 22, 1879. *The Letters of Gerard Manley Hopkins to Robert Bridges*, p. 79.

11. Letter to Robert Bridges, Feb. 10, 1888. *The Letters of Gerard Manley Hopkins to Robert Bridges*, p. 272. The poem in question is "Tom's Garland," a poem for which Hopkins had to send Bridges a "crib."

12. "As kingfishers catch fire, dragonflies draw flame," lines 2–3.

13. "The Wreck of the *Deutschland*," line 7.

14. Qtd. in Gerald Roberts (ed.), *Gerard Manley Hopkins: The Critical Heritage* (London: Routledge and Kegan Paul, 1987), p. 345.

15. Letter to Robert Bridges, Nov. 26, 1882. *The Letters of Gerard Manley Hopkins to Robert Bridges*, p. 163.

16. Letter to Robert Bridges, Apr. 3, 1877. *The Letters of Gerard Manley Hopkins to Robert Bridges*, p. 38.

17. For more on *cynghanedd* and its influence on Hopkins, see Glyn Jones, "Hopkins and Welsh Prosody," *Life and Letters Today* Vol. 21 (June 1939), 50–4; W. H. Gardner, "Gerard Manley Hopkins as a Cywyddwr," *Transactions of the Honorable Society of Cymmrodorion*, session 1940, pp. 184–8; Gweneth Lilly, "Welsh Influence in the Poetry of Gerard Manley Hopkins," *Modern Language Review* XXXVIII (July 1943), 192–205; A. Thomas, "Hopkins, Welsh and Wales," *Transactions of the Honorable Society of Cymmrodorion*, session 1965, pp. 272–85; and Gwyneth Lewis, "Extreme Welsh Meter," *Poetry* 205.2 (Nov. 2014), 162–71.

18. T. S. Eliot, *After Strange Gods: A Primer of Modern Heresy* (London: Faber and Faber, 1934), p. 47.

19. Ashley Brown, "An Interview with Elizabeth Bishop," *Shenandoah* 17 (Winter 1966), 3–19.

20. Karen V. Kukil, ed., *The Unabridged Journals of Sylvia Plath* (New York: Anchor, 2000), p. 224.

21. Ibid., p. 215.

22. Sylvia Plath, *Collected Poems*, ed. Ted Hughes (New York: Harper and Row, 1981), pp. 29–30.

23. Dennis O'Driscoll, *Stepping Stones: Interviews with Seamus Heaney* (New York: Farrar, Straus and Giroux, 2008), p. 37.

24. "As kingfishers catch fire, dragonflies draw flame," lines 3–4.

The World Is Charged:

Poetic Engagements with Gerard Manley Hopkins

WIN BASSETT

The Kings of Missoula

Thank you, oh merciful professor of poetry and trout
for the silvers, pinks, browns, and greens,
yellows, blacks, whites, and keen
eyes sensing fate after the flies haul bodies
from the world into depths unknown.

Perhaps a twist here, jiggle there will shake them back
to home. They learn wrestling with destiny is for naught.
Listen, now, to the verses flowing
beneath the rocks. God's words take them home.

LIBBY BERNARDIN

And the Great White Pelicans

lifted themselves with such
grace that I felt some blessing fall upon us
from the black-tipped wings gathering air,
pulling themselves away from earth
as though a white shawl
had shook itself,
then folding back in the wind, took our breath
from us with long orange-yellow beaks,
then circled back, on Marsh Island
on ocean shore, sand, grass,
mystical feet gathered into some
300 count of white plumage—
magnificent restless stalking,
we unwilling to leave what we were given
so that turning away, our hearts stirred
by the true splendor of a thing,
I stared longingly over our wake,
nothing illusory in the parting white foam,
nothing unreal in the beating wings.

ALLEN BRADEN

Inspiration

Not far from where a coyote led me
over the sparsely timbered hillside,
I found a feather held in the sagebrush
flanking an abandoned logging road.
I knew the pattern, its bars of tan
almost the color of parchment
or more like that coyote's pelt actually.
The feather of a great barred owl.
You could say the darker, narrower
scribbles curving toward the quill
suggest rows of silhouettes in flight.
You could say a lesson might exist
in the wind's subtle dispersal of dust
trickling through Sheepskull Gap,
estranging that feather from its wing.
All you really need to tell anyone
is how a single feather was poised
so the tip of the quill wrote on thin air.

Taboo against the Word Beauty,
Ornithological Version on Aesthetic Theory

Out of its craw, out of its flimsy trellis
of rib and cords of tendon, out of live flesh
copiously puckered by dark quill darkly
so iridescent,

the red-winged blackbird fashions its art. From wind
shuttling among warm mirages of marsh,
from air sizzling inside its instrumental
lungs, an orchestra

is engineered to orchestrate the thermals
caressing your body just now. Tomorrow?
Yesterday? Neither of sheer consequence here:
climactic moment

of neither coming nor going, when breath ends,
before song begins.

Bearded Barley

Proud and skinny tow-head
stretching for sunshine,

slender arrow of gold
or wand with stiff whiskers,

you offer us summer magic
out of water, dirt and light.

The millstone, the baker,
the slave, pulpit and priest,

they all send their regards.
You send back your straw

so they may build empires
and pray for your safe-keeping

when a cloudburst in August
bows you flat against the earth

below the teeth of the combine,
even the sickle's blade and cradle;

or when a twister drives you
clear through a telephone pole;

when the unbelievable seems true.
I could have sworn I saw you

hopping a train for the mill,
determined on being refined

into a loaf of bread or angel food
or maybe even the body of Christ.

STEVEN COLLIER BROWN

The Bowerbirds

I lean my chair against the pine.
The grass, with its late mow,
bares a bird's intaglio
of bones, blue glass, incarnadine
yarn. In the Frontyardless Age
of errant mowers out of sum,
I imagine some other me, my thumb
shaping stag gods in sludge
or stacking cairns. Then the wait—
inside a house without a door,
not knowing what I'm waiting for,
and the yard so wholly maculate.

The Small Bang

I could turn against my learning
here, rub away the Pentateuch,
brush it from the brainwall
for all the good it's done.
The swallow-washed woods
are damage-dipped—days'
flit litter since nothingness
startled into weight and depth.
At dawn: the exodus of ants
clasp at pips of sap.
At noon: the beetles unsleep,
stir old folioles to laughter.
Somewhere else: a darkness
coming on loud as song. O
Hylidae, swell me in thy chord.
Firefly clap me in thy spark.

ROBIN CHAPMAN

Dappled Things

Always the world-spun light casts patterns
raveled through the wind-thrown clouds, the forest's
branch-broken loom, across the hoof-scraped moss
and snow-banks, the backs of browsing mule deer
whose swiveling ears listen for the whispered sound
of the tawny cougar's padding walk. Dark and light,
sleep and wake and dream course through our lives
to make us what we are—sun and shadow-clothed,
bedrock and layers of fertile soil, green climb
and blight of history, wind-taken, time-wound
and wounded, heart-bound to world's warp and weft.

Fire

Out of dream sleep, deep sleep,
dawn embers flare, rinsing star sky,
setting shadows fleeing across
the landscape that wakes now not
to sun's single eye but cloud-breath,
leaf sigh, soaked field, spider-web;
dowsed light igniting mist, tree,
the woman bending to the weed-work
of day.

Landscape

What's native? This stretch of yard once marsh
fringed by tall-grass prairie, fire-swept, drained
to re-emerge in cherry, hickory, oak all felled
for lumber, fallow in winter, tilled to cornfield
fringing the edge of town—come house, grass,
elms, honeysuckle border creeping in—now
we machete-slash the stems of indigo, beebalm,
asters and goldenrod for slow compost, clear
so that the tender crocus, scilla, and daffodils
will lift their faces through leaf drift to the early
bees and each of us weary of winter sleep.

Spare

I watch the black crow, wing-wrenched,
walking on snow—how we can go on,
go on, memory-borne, through cold,
through wind's work, loved world,
till owl-dusk or fox-dawn. I want to walk
with my friends through broken-winged days,
want words to lift us back to the ordinary air,
to spare us pain. I want the words, when time
comes, to speak by our graves, to comfort
the living, honor the dead, lay each of us to rest
earth-borne, shroud-wound or wind-kissed,
grateful for life's brief flight of joy, light-blest.

MORRI CREECH

The Language of Pastoral

—FOR SUSAN LUDVIGSON

1.

I am halfway between the canebrake and the pines.
The horizon stretches like a bow-string, sun
deep citron over the pasture. Language whines
and lisps toward meaning, trying to get one
blessèd thing right—O wonders turned to signs:
trees shine with mold out where the creekbeds run,
wet fields brim with midges, and white curds
of foam wash up at the pond's edge in these words.

2.

Like spells to conjure with, this verb, this noun—
three red-winged blackbirds at the pasture's edge
gleaning the grass seed have already flown
and disappeared somewhere beyond the hedge,
only to be recalled in this phrase, set down
as a part of speech. So language keeps its pledge.
I find the loss in what these words redeem,
like the sleeper who awakes to another dream.

3.

I have come back in the middle of a sentence
in middle life: here my grandfather tended
corn and plowed the back fields, stripped the dense
kudzu before it choked the soybeans. Winded,
he'd walk along the full length of the fence
to drink cold water where the creekbed ended.
I imagine seeing him climb the distant hill.
Language sings its one song, *hold still, hold still.*

4.

What I have to say turns the pasture to fiction.
Parsing the back fields, grammar and syntax fail.
Even the blackbirds are reduced to diction,
sculling through air as they do above the swale.
A world combusts to nothing in the friction
between a phrase and its referent: or the tale
persists as cadence, though the names of things
are frail as spent breath or the midges' wings.

5.

Whom or what are these words for? Not the dead
who cannot hear them anyway. Not the wet
soybean fields or canebrake or the red-
winged blackbirds slurring the air. What slips the net
of language has no use for what is said
about it. Even I will soon forget.
Each word quarrels with silence at the close:
where speech comes from, and where everything goes.

6.

It is dark as I write this. The fields are far away.
Maybe the pasture hums with midges, reeds
teem at my grandfather's fenceline, and a stray
blackbird lifts toward the hill, beak full of seeds.
Maybe, for all the words I have had to say,
someone sits alone in a room and reads
in silence a poem beginning with these lines:
I am halfway between the canebrake and the pines…

At Buck Hall

—FOR SCOTT ELY

1.
Like dipping oars the egret strikes its wings
on the black water out near Pimlico,
scanning for those widening, dimpled rings
where fish break water, talons skimming low
over the shoals. An itch for landscape brings
me back here to these wetlands in the slow
half light of afternoon. Loose threads of day
spin themselves out in what I have to say.

2.
To shape coherence from that far company—
harrier hawk circling above the swales,
white tail scrambling across the thorns and scree
of the slick limestone berm. My eyesight fails
to knit it whole. Unlike the owl in its tree
that sees even a least twitch in the cattails,
I patch together buck, scree, briar, and bird
as best I can in the clear light, word by word.

3.
Such distance between what the eye takes in
and what the tongue gives back in its puzzle and sift,
sorting the mayflies from the dazzled spin
of oak leaves flashing silver. In the rift
between idea and flesh a brown marsh wren
flittering from a paper birch, too swift
for vision to hone in, grows still, having lit
here in the space this phrase has made for it.

4.
Suppose the sayer changes what he sees,
or makes a marsh wren up for story's sake
when a tanager, in fact, wings through the breeze
to cross the sawgrass shallows by the lake,
having flown from a stand of fictive trees.
What if this word-stitched landscape is a fake?
For all my honest effort, lies are hidden
in the pretense of each sentence I have written.

5.
Think how the visible becomes a dream
when, by some quirk of thought, a beech leaf stirs
and turns into a fawn's ear, or a stream
glints like a fish's scales. The mind conjures
the world to artifice, skews *be* to *seem*
in wild pursuit of meaning. What endures
—a paradigm in which the marsh wren flies—
is truer still for being a disguise.

6.
The shank end of late afternoon goes on
about its business heedless of the sounds
language has made of it. In a pond frogspawn
festers and reeks. A hare near the levee bounds
deep in the blackberry vines. When I am gone
egret and hawk will carry on their rounds.
And so will I, at my desk, when the day has passed,
setting it down in these words to make it last.

CAROLYN CREEDON

Pied Beauty

Glory be to the guy who invented Missouri for money,
with its plateglass heat, its thick-tressed storms,
its power outages, its broken water mains;
glory be to these broken-up brick stoops full of women who sit
calicoed, bandannaed, laughing and fanning at their men
making finger v-signs with light and dark roughened hands
who pull in from the Shop 'n Save and haul out silver bags of ice
from their Ford F-lines and pass them around;
glory be to Cedric's Fish Fry for cooking up everything
over a lit trash can before it all goes bad, glory to the beer
to be drunk while it's still cool, glory be to the E felony
of freeing the over-full fire hydrant, feeling the loose damp shirt
on the body; glory be to wearing nothing much, dancing with strangers,
glory be to someone's six-pack of D batteries, for the flashlights,
for the boom boxes blaring the bleats of poetry, a band called pain,
glory to the little girl with the doll tucked football-style under her arm,
its boy hair crisped sleek in the middle, two like waves meeting each to each,
glory to her mommy, whose feet hurt, who's home now
whose love for this girl in this place makes her skin feel raw and soft;
glory for half a moon that haloes everybody the same this night
for the nest of debris and leaves we rest on, and later, in the hot dark,
while I wave a lazy magazine, glory to the found matches you touch
to our Mary and Jesus industrial candles, lighting up
your sweat-dabbed glorious face;
para que no me atormenten de nuevo sino que seamos salvajes en la gloria del espiritu santo.
Praise this.

PHILIP DACEY

A Dream of Hopkins

He came close, kissclose, naked and transformed.
His body lit, seemed so, from within. No
Priest nor poet now but thin—thank sorrow—
Man. Around his fleshglow fell shadows swarmed.
Then he did this: rocked. Rude. Like a ship stormed.
And pointed, one hand high, the other low,
At himself. Heart and loins. Pure pity. Though
In such selflight looked at once harmed, unharmed.
O, and was silent, not: not to say but be
He came a—watch!—word, what someone—who?—spoke.
Wrote? A one-word book to read, ever. See:
Skin, bones (scored, skewered) shine outloud: *We broke*
Down, then out in praise. Now keep a mystery
Bodied forth. Have, give us. And then I woke.

A Simple Garden Ladder:

From the Lost Correspondence of Gerard Manley Hopkins to Robert Bridges

Imagine: two men, naked, and a ladder,
Opened to a tall A. No place in particular,
Rather a dark abstraction from place.
The ladder, wood, worn, stands grounded here, sure,
Yet yearns, by pointing, upward. The most
Remarkable the men, who ascend, descend
The steps, slow or leaping, acrobats, no,
Trans-acrobats, more than mere technicians,
Under the bar of the A, with bow, with crawl,
Between legs to enter and issue therefrom,
Or grapple, with the thing itself, hang, twist
Upon it, rack, riddle, and with each
Other as well, wrestle, to wring out breath
Or admission (even sometimes separately
With only, alone, earnest, themselves), sweat
All through this their shining badge. How lit?
Imagine this, then, Robert, and you have
My dream of nights ago. Or some of it:
There were innuendoes, shades and auras.
It stays and stays, as if not yet am I awake.

Who were they? Wild they were. In weak moments
I meditate upon those men, their ladder. Was it
Theirs? Possession by torment? It was, too, a
Tool. Whose, though? Another's they use, uses them?
Jacob and Esau, yes. But Esau saw no ladder.
Nor did they wrestle, only Jacob with
An angel. These took the place of angels,
Trafficked the vertical, heaven to earth
And reverse, yet were most clearly men, sexed,
No denying that. Their parts both were and were
Not part of the dream-dance without music:
Swinging freely in the sourceless light,
Seemed accompaniment, mere, for the moves
Of the whole bodies, and yet seemed also
What the whole bodies moved around
(Or the bodies, to be whole, moved around).
Circle-center to circumference.
                              But why

Two? I thought of man divided, even
Christ divided. Between here and there
The dark earth we take as lover, falling,
The sky, dark, if differently, if beautiful,
Appalling. But no, none of that will do,
Is too simple: these men of mine hung once
Upside down, feet hooked on upper rungs, hands
Grazing ground, so that direction was lost,
In going up they seemed to be going down,
Sky rode low under the flying earth, or seemed to,
I was as lost as North and South. Nor was one
Light the other dark in easy opposition, were twins
(Like Jacob and Esau), their fate shared, I woke
As together they lifted the ladder onto
Their backs (or was I still lost, and it
Was the ladder carried them away?).
                                        Dare
I, Robert, even for laugh, suggest they
Were we? At serious play between
Pride and prayer? Or in debate about my
Faith, the Jesuit ideal (you disapprove; thus,
As I, in my terms, mount, or would, you see
My sad decline). But their bodies were similarly
Trim; ours are no such pair: you, long athletic,
Show it; bare, I am poor, minimal, boy-bodied.
If I watched us, we were in disguise.
Whatever it was I watched was in disguise.

Still, I know this much: it was a simple
Garden ladder. To climb upon to pick
Fruit from a tree. In looking back I am surprised
It was so simple a thing. It seemed so much more.
Though I can't say for certain now, it it-
self might have been the very source of light,
In memory it feels so. Ladder-light
By which I saw the bodies of men.
By which they saw each other and themselves.

The Sleep

"I AM SO HAPPY."
   —The final, death-bed words of G. M. H.

It is an answer, a going-into.
The soft helmet slowly eases over the head.
The limbs begin to believe in their gravity,
The dark age of faith begins, a god below
Draws down the body, he wants it
And we are flattered.
We are going to the level of water.
(Don't hold on. Drop fair, drop fair.)
This is a fine seepage, we think,
Seepage ravelling to a river
To set ourselves upon. So
What is the price of dark water?
Where is the weight going?
The body powers the vaguest of shapes,
Pilot-boat, the falls collapse
And collapse upon themselves. We hear them
In time and imitate them.
We would turn to water that has lost
Its floor, water surprisingly
In space and beading,
A glittering disintegration.

            Now, what was a bed
Rocks just perceptibly, this is a cradle
In search of a captain, the bone-cargo
Settles, the medium
Washes up over and across and fills
The spaces we have been keeping empty just for this,
The palpable black herein
Barbarian, riding us down.

            There will be a level
We come to, will we know it?
A flat place with, look, a light.
It is a guess as our loins give way.
Already we are forgetting
Where we were
And left from, the human

Faces like sunglare hurting our eyes.
Did we even say goodbye? Yet could there
Possibly be someone here now,
That this going down
Not be so sole, and sore,
A cup, a cupped hand, a basket,
These forms of containment
Forms of Person
Where, when we're water, we're caught?
Listen. It is the sound of ourselves,
This passage: a breath.
We are almost not here.
If we break up this softly,
We must be incomparably lovely.

MEG DAY

Ghazal for My Selves, as Samson & Delilah

NO, I'VE REALLY HIT THE JACKPOT.
 —*James Baldwin, when asked, "Has being gay been a disadvantage?"*

I am the woman about whom my mother warned me: dangerous
& philistine. I have tempted truth into the honeyed light of day

from the thorax of a lion and fed it, with my fists, into sorrowed mouths
whose fertile worry hives in the ears of girls like vagrant dayflies

to keep them from slumber that might steal their hair. Some of us are born
supernatural: some of us wake to find the secrets we shared were daydreams

instead, pollinated by fear. I need not say I killed the lion: I need only remember
the sweetness of surprise in place of my mane. Let me introduce you to daylight:

it was my hands that held the shears, my mouth the comb. I have never been
unclean. Pull the pillars down around my chest at the first sign of daybreak,

& tuck me in to that blanket of stone. O, that you would make me feeble,
asleep upon your knee! That I was born to love this weakness as I do the noonday

shade. Cup your hand to the stubble of my skull, the sticky underneath: out of the eater,
something to eat and out of the strong, something gentler still: every day

I wake still warm and breathing. I never mourn the muscle lost. Forget foxes, or flame: I
am the son about whom my lover was warned would feed the night to day.

Aubade for One Still Uncertain of Being Born

Lie still. Make their desperate hunt for your heart
beat them frenzied & let them second-guess
your muted tempo as counterfeit for their own.
Press your palm, still learning to unfurl,
to your den's wet beams & steady yourself
against the doorjamb of your lair; it will be time
when it is time. If your mother is a horse—& I am,
I am—let her approach Troy with you still hidden
within. Let her carry you like a bouquet of splinters
in her belly of timber still hot from hatching
at the future for firewood like it was a family tree.
All your life they will surround you, will stalk & strain
to hear that ballad from your canary pipes, will tempt
your quiet cover, will kick the keg of your desire
until it is dented nameless; all your life they will try
to say you are built for something else. It begins now—
so hush, hush: be nothing, just this once.

R. H. W. DILLARD

Curtal Sonnet (with an Admonition)

Sonnet starts (not P or S, but G
        MH, this one, called curtal ((one sestet,
                Quatrain and tail)), unusual), begins
(H whom Yeats met but forgot ((how we
        Should take note, pay heed, recall, lest that
                We too become just an anecdote, intend

It or not, (((yes, met him once or twice
        But scarcely noticed, must have missed it,
                How he looked, sounded, thick or thin,
Tall or short, rude, nasty, maybe nice)))))
        But whose poetry we remember).
                                Sonnet ends.

LYNN DOMINA

Confession to Hopkins

Yes, our great world bends to fit her warm breast,
her long bright wing curving across seas, skimming
hillsides, sun-soaked, shaded, every slope
drawn toward her downy glide. She alights
in a village, within a cluster of girls
beading bracelets at the edge of a field. They watch her
as they would watch a feral cat or porcupine,
curious, wary. I'm wary too,
of my own longing—could such soft feathers
ever brush the curve of my shoulder, pause,
invite my repose? Would I then feel
the thrum of her breast thrumming in my throat,
knowing how great was my fear, how immense my desire?

GEORGIA EDWARDS

Come to Me

You call for me—O come to me,
I scatter your tears on the lintel beam.
Your will, want-weary, pounds
stacked stone deaf—sealed
old wood silent, still.

Windswell swift whistles
your wings, launches
you trembled over garden walls
that only grow in graces given
least's lowered gaze. You circle
comfort-cold, light-blind,
like starving bats looped in flight,
world-worn, breath-empty—

And you call to me—O come to me—
I rest for you in the dogwood tree—
petals fanned full in compass rose.

DESMOND EGAN

Hopkins in Kildare

DELIVERED AT HOPKINS'S GRAVE, GLASNEVIN, JUNE 16TH 1989
ON THE CENTENARY OF HIS DEATH.

Father Gerard at rest among your brethren
almost anonymously as you would have wished
with only pebbles to pick out your five foot two

your life the poetry water and wine
have so real a presence since that we
taste one in tasting the other
as we lay in Glasnevin a 100 year garland
lily and iris for man and poem together
Elected silence! sing to me…
Summer ends now, now barbarous in beauty the stooks…
Margaret are you grieving
Over Goldengrove unleaving?

and through lines you willed us we may glimpse
a face gone pale with thinking a head too large
for a build slight as Beckett's
the English fingers the unreachable
melancholy of the artist
as we converge in tribute to our more than friend
and to your convert's almost medieval search for
certainties none of us dare expect
since we are all *time's eunuchs*
though you broke into wholeness at the end
and died like Simeon *so happy*

now as I commune here with the maker
of poems that will always make a difference
I see your pale face eyeing from a carriage
out of the puffing and clanking into
the Victorian station of Newbridge
catching at the accent of this remove
or arriving at your destination
black a black Jesuit suitcase some
volume in hand a theme and
walking slowly along the canal
breathing-in the place the bog air

its lost century the water above water
the rhythm of little Ireland opening in lock gates
and smiling through shyness when old Miss Cassidy
steps out to greet you opposite the very beech
where Father Prendergast was hanged

or genuflecting in surplice before the tabernacle
in the apse of St. Peter's and Paul's
as you carry a ciborium for the rail of Kildare faces
to distribute with unsteady hand your last Christmas

or years earlier gone solemn among confrères
tense with vocation sitting for a Clongowes photo
uneasy with any place of honour

or looking-up from the breviary your hair going grey
to study that suddenness of Athlone its east and west
opening along the wide river

or again on retreat at Rahan
pacing your soutane trying to avoid conversation
with trees our midland cloud one blade of grass

and I can see your imprisoned stare from
that top storey of St. Stephen's Green
biting at a finger a black sonnet gnawing
into a scrawl more lines for nobody
with that almost desolate look towards your Gardens

martyr of silence
wanting o so badly to turn
weightless as a line to
hover sweep fly free rise on a thermal
into the infinite heavens
yet able to say *justus quidem tu es Domine*
when living was plodding and plodding
your steadying gaze has turned into inspiration has
unconvered the audience you hid
in that future where your spirit might breathe

in people like us
who admire too your holy indifference
your quiet which pierces this empire of noise
to mould things into themselves

your spirit darts through our human June

JOHN FREEMAN

August Green: A Baptism

A gap in privet led from a mowed field
   to the floor of a leaf pavilion
     so thick that every shade was green:
   the air was stained olive, the shafts of light
     chartreuse. I stood in a dripping heat
where I could not belong, thought it fathered all with root.

I had trespassed on the most ancient of temples, where green
     reaches up to the answering spirit of light.
   I dreamed of sharing with tree and vine
     the mysteries of communion,
to grow from within where the sun's finger touches the leaf.
   But sweat stinging my eyes and skin,

     horsefly, mosquito, and gnat
harried me back through the gap into open field.
   I squinted as wind dried my sweat,
feeling restored in a way I could not name
   but to say the light had watered
     something within me deeply green.

Birds at Dawn

In the false dawn
my campfire is the only light.
I stoke it against the cold.
Before daylight, birdsong
kindles from all around
till the dark smolders with their sound.

The rudiments of light crack
the horizon like an opening eyelid.
Still invisible, birds are on the move
trailing wakes of lyric
I remember but can't identify
through the formless darkness of the sky.

Light slowly hardens into vision.
Glory blinds the edges of clouds.
At last I see them, follow them on the wing—
red-tailed hawks balanced like balsa planes,
dive-bomber catbirds,
cartwheels of martins, sparrows porpoising—

birds which had been sound become sight
as the mind solves the riddles of the heart.

ALICE FRIMAN

The Acolyte

And the fire that broke from thee then
—*Hopkins*

Spring, and the birds are flocking,
revved up and zooming
around the house in a sleeve
of air, bouncing off windows
then pouring into the holly tree
to gorge on red berries. Wee
gray engines with brown tufts
too wet out of the shell for
thoughts of wooing. Only eating
and being part of the vow that is
each other. Born to it, this watery
flow of multiple births moving as one—
this communal orgy of worship.

The holly is Argus-eyed,
each berry, each holy tidbit
winking red, signaling
from dark leaves: Eat me, stuff me in,
shit me out. Spread the good news.

But what of the celebrant
too heavy with bliss, too loaded
with gobble and gulp, who hit
the window? The *ah! bright wings*
that never rose? The baby dinosaur
blessed with appetite, slammed
by a boomerang of light?
I tell you, *My heart in hiding*
Stirred for a bird. The split breast.
The stained feathers. Gash. Gush
of red spill. Splotch of sour and unripe.

TAYLOR GRAHAM

To a Young Poet Resisting Hopkins

Don't even try to understand the logic of a rhyme
that rises on wing-feather to achieve lift of line.

Song is what takes hollow bone and makes a wing,
leading edge of wing, wind-hover adrift of line.

Blind-bright sun on feathers will give shape
to flight. Translate that, its fine sift of line.

Now you have music. Meaning springs from language
like a fledgling full-formed on the shift of line.

Here's longing sprung from brooded egg, broken
empty shells, the bare-bone body, shrift of line.

Take flight, leave the shell behind. Unfurl
these wings to sail, spendthrift of line.

JESSE GRAVES

Arrhythmia

The word so musical Hopkins
might have invented it,
inscape of the body's cavity,
thisness felt in quick flutters.

Noticing nothing is normal,
constant rhythm so regular,
so boring, it slides past.
Until suddenly it doesn't,

sprung rhythm of blood
and synapse surging
fast down through the arms,
fingers seizing to catch

whatever seems slipping away.
Then you'll know it, such
soft sputtering, quivering
like the gills of a hooked fish.

Goldengrove

We drift though the back fields,
father and daughter, weekend visitors,
strolling where I was raised.
In the shallow folds of the wood,
bones flare up in the sun
like struck match-heads,
picked clean and scattered
across the open meadow.
The child knows we can never
put these pieces back together,
reassemble the young heifer lost
while calving, death within a death.
The girl's eyes announce that we
shall not leave the unburied
littered among brambles and briars,
shadows of the leafless oak grove.
Because sorrow's springs are the same
forever, we gather the fragments
and build a drumlin of bones,
halcyon home to the wind,
or shelter for any wayward bird,
wings beating like a heart
behind a wall of bare ribcage.

EVE GRUBIN

Date

Not through a kiss but through his solitary gaze
slanting when I lifted my hair wet-heavy with downpour

heaped it on top of my head elbows pointing neck tilted the meat
restaurant window bleared

with water smeared beaded with dust and haze we talked
Malamud and Rashi and forgiveness

the Jewish way a letting go of blame because we are not the final judge
how it's freeing "liberating" he said his gaze lay

agitated on the bend between my shoulder and chin what is
a single look? what is *seeing*? how it digs hard horse hooves striking

dry ground a smack against your chest stoned
from soup hot in my throat and his eyes

regarding the skin just above my clavicle rain
plunged hard behind his round glasses and black skullcap

pounding the umbrellas and gutters and later
that week my friend told me he'd said to her "I could

tie you to the bed" when I heard that it was as if
I had already heard it soup-heat blushed my tongue his look

searing my collarbone I tell you his eyes flared
as if his troubled intellectual mouth tied me

LUKE HANKINS

All Fall Long

I can feel fall
and a falling feeling—
feeling The Fall
and what was fallen from
in the cool air—
both foreign and familiar.
And the feeling comes on,
falling through me, and rising,
rousing me, awe-full all fall long.

MARYANNE HANNAN

Strife

HE SHALL COVER THEE WITH HIS FEATHERS,
AND UNDER HIS WINGS SHALT THOU TRUST
    Psalms 91, 4

Under what Paracletian wings
do our piteous petitions ricochet
fantastically, sheer off vastness?
What folds unfathomed
cover dark writhings, mirthless
revelry, while we wrestle
roughshod rubble? While we
tender our trust to others?

JEFF HARDIN

The Bounds of Belief

"THERE LIVES THE DEAREST FRESHNESS DEEP DOWN THINGS."
—*Gerard Manley Hopkins*

Dearest?
　　　　Anymore, such language
　　　　　　　　runs the risk

　　　　　　of being called extreme,
　　　　　　　　grandiose, too certain of itself,
　　　　　　　　　　bold beyond the bounds of belief,

　　　quaint even—maybe, in some circles, reckless. Any

freshness
　　　　there might have been
　　　　　　has long since turned stale.

　　　　　　Doesn't the hunger still remain, though,
　　　　　　　　the ache, the reaching up
　　　　　　　　　　out of ourselves,

　　　　the palm at the end of the mind? Isn't there some deeper

deep
　　　　than what our words
　　　　　　can touch,

　　　　　　some farther far?
　　　　　　　　Where is lightheartedness?
　　　　　　　　　　Where joy, conviction, purpose?

　Where plenitude of spirit, leaping about? Let's get

down
        to the bedrock
                to see if one exists,

           to say a final yes or no.
              In the light of last lights,
                     in this bent and broken world,

can there be wings brooding over us or the teaching of all

things
        honest and just, lovely
                and pure? Is uncertainty

           our only certainty? Suppose questions
            are only stall tactics
                  delaying an answer. What can that

mean for us, charged as we are to seek what everything means?

The Mind and Soul Growing Wide Withal

"Like,"
        the kids say now,
                over and over,

                or click on Facebook—
                        small affirmations
                                that can't fully explore

        the knitted souls of vehicle and tenor, the glimpsed-forth

shining
        of one thing seen
                through the presence

                of another. In the way
                        that the self more clearly
                                understands

        where it is now by seeing through the lens of where it came

from.
        One person needs another
                to see past

                the mind, to conceive
                        what's possible
                                even to conceive.

        One tense needs another: is/was, shake/

shook,
        to rattle the insides
                of what we think

                we think, what we
                        know we know,
                                what we don't know

        we don't know or can't know. Through Laertes'

foil

      we better grasp

            the questions of Hamlet.

        "The inward service

           of the mind and soul

               grows wide withal,"

he says, and we enter ourselves fully, not *only* ourselves.

DAVID HAVIRD

The Horse on Zennor Hill

...THAT HIGH HORSE RIDERLESS,
THOUGH MOUNTED IN THAT SADDLE HOMER RODE
   —*W. B. Yeats*

Amid the yellow gorse, which pricked my jeans,
and purple foxgloves and bluebells—
puddles of hoofprints,
the footpath in places trampled to mire,
and not a horse to be seen.
Even when I reached the granite tor,
and the green high moor with its boulders,
swept by the wet benumbing wind from seaward,
widened before me, none to be seen.

Where were the words, the pages whipping back
and forth, in which the poet lies
on Zennor Carn *In a bower of bramble?*
Lies only in words,
having no bed, much less a grave
marked by any one
of these abraded boulders—
or, better, marked by this, a block
of granite, the one stone owing its shape to hands,
a monument to those that quarried the site
and dismantled the cairns. Where was the horse,
wings furled—within which one?

Above the spires of the fox
Gloves and above the bracken
Tops with their young heads
Recognizing the wind
(the boulders unmindful), a kestrel hovered,
circled and hovered, its shrill two notes
lost to the ear, caught by the wind straightway.
I'd set his words by saying them aloud
in stone, in this whose form evokes,

while granite is softening atom by obdurate atom,
a wind with hands to coax the stone
that's stubborn by design to foal.

for W. S. Graham (1918–1986)

AVA LEAVELL HAYMON

The Tao of Alphabet

Joy is the first part of join
yet if the n snaps on too neatly
        joy is soon (and so on) gone.

that same pesky n
unmakes the bed
so joy could bend
and entwine

till what's previous is precious
        The tiny twin lines join and

        the danger is anger (as always)

the d coming off
with a distinct *tink*
and circling back to GO
in the eternal search for God.

But even God doesn't last long
        (all things are in flux), our protection
against flu the signature of an illiterate.

God reshuffles to dog. As we giggled
in 5th grade, joy and change
made school yard swings
of wings and sod.

Winter Mother

We've left the crib, the family
animals, the unstable first trinity.
Forgiven the all night journeys

made in haste, the rough beds,
the secrets and baffling dreams. Since
our father left us, his words

in our ears orate a baritone
poetry, wild and strong enough
to hold the yes and the no.

Again the sun leans toward its death
and our mother grows small.
Her forehead curves under

our hands like a child's.
In her daughters' touch
she finds babies,

long birth, the stars and songs.
Before its end, her life blooms into myth.
She will leave behind attar of roses,

a portrait on blue fabric, her face
in the cliffs. We live and we die
but she will be assumed,

we are certain, like goddesses
everywhere. She waits. She will light
the clouds in her long passage.

Feast of Guadalupe, Dec 12

JANE HICKS

My Second-Grade Teacher Reads Us Gerard Manley Hopkins

At art time, we crafted Christmas paper, careful-kept,
reborn as tissue kites. Tethered rainbows with tattered tails
climbed into March, darted and leapt over playground minions.

A hawk on thermals glided, soared, swooped among the kites,
winged away, climbed high to wheel and hover, all below transfixed.
Back inside, teacher plucked a book from her shelf of verse,
"Listen with your heart," she said. "Ride the words
like a hawk rides the wind or kites dance free."

So I rode words that galloped on springs, swept off, soared again,
fell into now, cloaked in *vermilion*,
newest in my heart-cache of words.

JAN D. HODGE

A.M.: Her Lone Spark Dying

TO A WEEPING TEEN

Márgarét, dón't be gríeving
Just because Eugene is leaving.
Hé, líke a very man! You,
Young as yet, who's sadder thán you?
Déar, ás your heart grows older
It will come to such things colder
By and by, nor waste a sigh
When passing lovers wave good-bye,
Nor will you weep nor doubt why.
For no matter what his name,
Pléasure's fálls áre the same,
Though every heart and maiden breast
Longs to deny what you have guessed:
It ís the fate you were meant for,
Every woman you lament for.

THOMAS ALAN HOLMES

Ascension

When pulling poison ivy, partway through
a day in May, the morning middling warm,
I stood to find myself inside a swarm
of honeybees, the ones I'd spoken to
when I'd pass by the sassafras. Although
they buzzed and circled, I felt no alarm
for me, but reverie: for me, in form
the dying sassafras, the bees for you.
I've watched the notch, the twin trunk at fork's cleft
and worried what great split from storm or wind
might rive the hive, leave me forlorn, bereft,
until I saw remaining bees attend.
No sting so fierce as my first fear they'd left,
I'd seen a new-formed swarming queen ascend.

JAY HOPLER

That Necessary Evil

A church bells the birds

Over the roofs of Perugia and a blue haze in a gauze-fall
        sprawls out long
Along the walls; the sun

'S light hits not hard the hills, but holds
Them. Still—.

        And stills their green velocities

Until such time such sky it has attained that by its own wild
Rising are they unrestrained, and left to wester, rolling, fast

And shadow-

Less.

The End of the Happy Hours

A dog doth to itself give yelpèd bliss, but you and I are not such
    things as bliss, self-yelped, doth well suffice
These days. You know I don't have any money.
Isn't there a radio playing? If we walk from this bed to that chair,
    if we listen....Listen:
Our song is changing its snake bones.

———————————

What yelpèd bliss a dog doth give itself! If only you and I such
    screaming bliss possessed. Wouldn't it suffice?
Some day...no. We will never have any money.
But there is a radio playing. If we walk from this chair to that
    door, if we listen—. Listen:
Our only song has changed its bones.

RON HOUCHIN

One Wet Wednesday Afternoon

Digging in the backyard for the first time
outside the bounds of garden, I feel
earth not so dry, not so grainy,
like one substance from the soaking.

In her chair Mother naps and no one watches.
What might I find, once I tear the hide
of grass away? I claw down, deep
as I can reach. Something squishes

in my hand. What if I hold a hidden organ
of the quivering world? Before I can run
inside, rain freezes to nails, sun stumbles
and falls. Mountains, like scowling faces,

turn toward me. From what vital
bladder or skull, I dread, without such
words, have I squeezed bile, brain,
or the unknown heart of the day?

JOAN HOULIHAN

By Eye-slit

BY EYE-SLIT, by blood-drum, by clumsy pats   along your arm, by
bracing thighs and heaving up   you almost stood, but slumped.
I listen to you sleep, sawn limbs   whispering *wood* to the head,
an assemblage made of the parts   you came from.
There is someone else in this room, I said   as the ghost blew from my mouth,
made a taste bordering on burnt and   to your caved body
unfed, no end to its wound, went.   The home gone to is not this home.

Come on the Cold

COME ON THE COLD of autumn, they rain
as twisted soft, as wet to the root,
lower then low, where no animal can.
Piecemeal and venous and fluttered, they rain.
I have loved and served but mixed my breath
with the sound a lung makes in its lake of blood.
Where the calf leaves hoof-prints of milk
in the dirt, where fire is the boyhood of wood, his ash,
speckled and flimsy and spread without thought,
on house, on horse, on hearse, they rain.
I have loved with remorse, harness and pain.

No Fire

NO FIRE to autumn's oak,   apple-stray or leaf,
dipped instead in pitch: our life, the one we forged
(a forgery!) and stood beside.   No longer the summer
in which we lived,   calling each other home—
we are talked out, fallen   through, inside a machine
that nicks us sleepless, knowing   *cold* to mean a coming
frost, our winter, and   lost as talk on our tongues.
Bagged and tube-hung,   sacked, the skin a drape,
inward-stripped and junked   into a constant eddy
of blood, the sound of you   before your voice is gone.

Would Come Back

WOULD COME BACK tongued and talking, laughing off
the soot and small hallways where he had to crouch
and squirm to get through, not fearing close spaces
as when he lived, for all is puzzle, a game
to come on the clues: miniature dog in full point,
monogrammed robe, a globe, three screws
and an oscillator, mashed landscape from a train set—.
how does it all fit in? Now he has his brown study, all the quiet
he wants, and no one can distract him from his thought-
work, whirr and pulse of machine in machine, nobody
to bother him with origin or end, as if he has his first mind,
not his last. Without hand-hold or leg-hold, hearth-tender
and in full kilter, he would come and be the gathering in my head,
the grave inside I tend and tend, the one that is blackening soft.

JAMES CLINTON HOWELL

River, Dissolution

A Carolina spider lily hafts
through rock upon shale and water.
The garbulb shreds into blades
of infant cartilage when wind
tots back the stem,
dunks the lump upstream
to click on stone.

Love can only lose in this place.

Cecil tows Melba by cardigan to where
granite crops deepest,
lets go of her armless sleeves that
shimmer on current,
ghost oars in oarlocks.
Down she flows through county
farms, into the land's sunwhite memory.

He never hems back the bank,
leases land to summer floods.
His head loses the line stitching
day to calendar day.

In the shower he crumples on
tiles locked into grid,
skull full of water.

Mildew slashes caulk seams,
angles up the wall until
spore overflows, blots over plates,
scrim on old bone.

REBECCA GAYLE HOWELL

from *Four Common Prayers*

Because the snow had not come,
    winds not

Because your mouth was the mountain
    we walked
    your words, my words,
    the thin light-reaching trees

Because everything that lives was singing
    and we heard *rejoice rejoice*

      (though everything that lives was dying
                or dead and
                singing
                please)

Because I could not love you more,
    though I tried
    Fires of rose-hips and saffron
    Your mouth, a pyre   built
    by my two hands

Because of this, I sang
    though the ice was coming
    though all songs were air

And did you sing back?
    Chorus to chorus, refrain
    (funeral dirge, fugue—refrain)

Did you sing?

I could not hear you over the dry ground
    over cracks of flame
    the hawk feeding her screeching young
    the rat, being eaten

Here was the hour, here was the day:
    & I would not turn from my thoughts,
    my looping cadence call
    I would not hush

How worry ruins every
    love I would not
    stop

        I would not

Night—an infant suckling
    I once held her in the way mothers do
    happy to be the filth river that buoys her
    and that she was made to cross

Once your mouth was the ridge we walked
    and I was the dry grass singed
    I, the rat and the hawk
    All enemies   of and not of the flesh

    But now I'm too tired to give birth

Do you want to know how the snow came?
    The rains, for weeks the rains
    Green flooding streets and houses
    Floating buses, shoes, floating beds

The snow came the only way it could:
    when everything left

        and how I was afraid

KIMBERLY JOHNSON

Pater Noster

This garden is a miracle.
Aphids dropped with April, gorgeous emeralds
with teeth. They preen against the petals,
distill sweet sap to honeydew.

Down bark, down fencepost, tazzled branches
dart and pull their braiding shadows, a slapstick
of diffraction. Downwind the barnstormers
perfect their spectacle—stiff cloth, wood

prop, 2-cycle engine ascending like a prayer
to flame out, hang breathless, cartwheel
over and power swooping earthward.
It's all for show, the windswept scarf

from forties matinees, the smoky trail,
the drama of the stall. The pilot streaks
to level, tilts a greeting as he buzzes
overhead, milks the throttle, rolls

headlong into a spin, whining, frictive, the form
of glory, and gloriously sunstruck. Seasonal
the ritual, pinching aphids as I kneel
upturned, squinting sunward for the sleek

daredevil flight, for the promise of the climb,
of sunlit wings, of plain things charged
and fulgent, of one perfect
performance, of *earth as it is in heaven.*

Spring Again

The cardinals are in from the meadow,
sparking in the thicket. Ever misplaced,
ever immoderate of hue, they scuttle
in the aspens—sweep of wing, slight wake,
the leaves a clatter of silverlings. Bedewed,
the thatch underfoot sponges, the spider's web
spreads a screen of pearls.
                              In a hollow uphill
from the abandoned town, the water-table
tops the soil. Low the turlough
in its occasional bed, runoff-cold
and day-shadowed, flat glass
pressed into a slump of land.
It will leave the meadow matted when it drains.
Grasses strow the surface, mutinous grasses
stretch and bow along the ridge.

But you—no bird, no fuss of grasses, you—
a leathern, a tight coil of fibers,
a honey-throated shambles.
You are exquisite. You are better
left to the imagination, better in your traces:

the timber pitched against the incline angle,
postholes stitching the edge of the pasture,
a spill of granite at the quarry lip, your song
wording cardinal, turlough, and town,
and, at the mouth of the canyon, the flowers
cupped like pinnae, ground littered
with spilt seedpods, tender cotyledons
cracked and agape, and me, breaking
off flowers, saying their names:

Here is the blazing star. Here is the deer's ear
opening its tiny, white symmetry.
Here is the fireweed, green buds
breaking to red, a bouquet of soldering irons.

A Psalm of Ascents

1.

Rank and damp the vapors, backstaggering
out the greenhouse door for stricter soils
I set out, to instruct my looser soul

in the postures of piety. Forty
desert days should scorch my concupiscent
senses to meekness, swerve devotion

from this fond flesh, this riveting
shambles, toward some legible heaven.

2. *Death Valley*

The basin's rim absorbs with its basalt
the predawn gray. Heartbroken have I hastened
to this heartbroken place, most humble earth

knuckled beneath the reach of water, hot
as hell and godforsaken. Knuckling I
kneel into the gravel and brace for day.

3.

Sunrise in adagio, vastly pink
over the Hundred-Year Bloom, the sand waste
flush with primroses,
                          blown anemones,

verbena blaring in gold and purple,
scrolls of fiddleneck, a fallen sky
of golden aster
                  sticky aster
                                false

star
        star lily
                    Bethlehem lily.
Even the joshua's spikes are spiffed
with lilies.

4.

    Fuzzed with pollen, fat bees

nuzzle the desert's unaccustomed
frillery, nectared legs slick and swagging.
Outlandish busybodies, so far

from their apiary comforts, they stroke
the orchid's perverse opulence and fidget
the gravel in clusters, the dewy ground

beaded in sticky, waggling gold.

5.

With strange throats the cardinals gloat
over their luck *what-cheer-cheer-cheer*, their cheer
drooping in doppler retreat as they swoop

from me, ever from me further, red flight
into a field of color. I am caught
red-handed—no, red-*hearted* in flagrant

delight. My knees confess it, unbending
up from the razor gravel all bloodied
with primroses.

JOHN LANE

Poinsett's Bridge

Early fall, the first flush of full season's surge,
the air humming with coming frost, the hawk's hovering
on mountain front, cliff-climbers, cleft in clouds,
shadow over the sun, then fallen into wind's harness.

In the woods, history-hidden by vines and last leaves,
standing stone-bridge, still strong, steady, dry-stacked
time-blunt, dappled by days, dawn and dusk, lichen-thick,
hanging arch still looms, bat darkness toward the middle.

Stone masons tired with all the hauling, time's limpid
winded weary wandering way: harrier-hanging off Caesar's
Head, tilts in wind and drifts west, one more fall.

KEAGAN LEJEUNE

Reverdie

Maybe the splintered stick teaches the lesson,
maybe it's the snapping turtle's open maw,
maybe it's the show of thumb gone to that thresher,
finger to the hatchet block, knuckle to the saw.
Maybe it's the creature dead on the chicken coop
while we stoke the fire and watch water boil
or the man who shows us how the jaws,
though sour with death, are still sprung to fall.

No, stripped to our underwear, waist-deep
in the canal, it's the foot against the shell
that sets the truth like a fisherman's hook,
quickly in—too sheer and shining to dislodge:
Sumer is icumen in,
scuttling the bottom with tail and claw,
pregnant with the mud of deep down things,
patient in folds of skin, and beautiful, and barbed.

GWYNETH LEWIS

The Telegraph Baby

—1916

And now I remember the tall hussar
who gave me the halo of telegraph wire
which I wound round my body at the age of six.
Since then my hearing's been strangely acute,
for I watched as the workmen erected a line
of identical crosses all the way down
to the river that kept on discussing itself
out through the village, on to somewhere's sea.…
He was huge in his dolman and when he saw

my delight at the splitting and hewing of wood
he called me closer to his brilliant braid
then the world dipped and I could see the way
that men were cradled in the criss-cross tree,
hammering nonsense, till they left one man
like a Christ on the wire there, hanging alone
but listening to something that no one else heard.
My heart beat in dashes back down on the ground
and I knew that I'd learn how to understand

the metal's despatches. Now, since the war
I've crossed high passes to talk in Morse
to other transmitters, leading horses piled high
with the weight of talking, till I found my way
here to the trenches, to the news of troops,
disasters and weather, where now I'm stretched out,
nerves copper and all my circuits aware
they're transmitting a man on a wheel of barbed wire,
nothing but message, still tapping out fire.

Red Kites at Tregaron

They know where to find me when they want to feed.
At dusk I prepare, lay out the fat

and spread unspeakable offal in snow
like scarlet necklaces. They know

how to find me. They are my words
for beauty and other birds

fight them, vulgar, down threads of air
which bring them to me. They brawl for hair,

for skin, torn giblets and gizzard which I
provide for them, domestic. Inside

the house is so cold I can see my breath,
my face in the polished oak. My mouth

is sweet with silence. Talon and claw
are tender to me, the craw

much kinder than men. What is most foul
in me kites love. At night I feel

their clear minds stirring in rowan and oak
out in the desert. I stroke

the counterpane, my sleepless skies
filled with the stars of untameable eyes.

ED MADDEN

Ark

CHRISTMAS 1966

The small box is filled with little beasts—
a barn that's a barge, a boat—the ark's

ridged sides like boards, a plastic plank,
a deck that drops in fitted slots, but lifted

reveals that zoo of twos—heaped beasts
to be released beneath a glittering tree,

its dove-clipped limbs. Dad's asleep
in his reclining seat, and crumpled waves

of paper recede as Mom circles the room.
The humming wheel throws light across the walls.

Saint's finger, Hill of Slane

Almost stepped on it, on them, bits of digit,
a pinky, knuckle, in the grass and gravel, graveside,

no blood, just dust, grit, some wire in it, in them,
the fingers, bits fallen off, but it's the savior

not a leper, or perhaps St. Pat, some pope—don't know,
just that he's mythic, biblical, robed, and old

as these things go, though these tombs are newer than
the ruins all around—the stone he's propped on

a grave of the lately gone—he's chipped, maybe chapped,
grey saint, white-washed, waving his hand

like that, disfigured benediction for those damn kids
crawling the walls and up inside the old tower,

cider and crisps in the friary, butts, some fumbling
about the motte and bailey just beside, relics

left behind, like these knocked off parts
on the lawn, almost stepped on, those two

bent digits in the litter that say he was divine
and not, flesh like us, to be picked up, pocketed.

In the absence of a contract

A field of rings glistens in the pawnshop
like cold wickets on grey lawns—

like shackles fragile and under glass, locked
boxes, pincushions of love and loss. Pawned

white gold lifted, found—the old vows
around the ring ground down, the tux and gown

now dust, names polished away. Second hand,
it fits your hand. *Ecce homo*. He is the man.

MAURICE MANNING

Ten Penny

I like looking at something strange, like a nail
driven crookedly and bent
into a hard plank in the barn with the head
sort of lolling over and stiff. It's strange
to be sticking plainly out of the order
of the barn and to have a singular
countenance. But the barn itself
on the whole is not so rational—
it has a significant uphill lean,
which I admire or regard as I would
a statue in a church with a sad
and still compassionate face looking out.
Whoever drove the nail got it
only to go so far before
it bent, and then he hit it again
and further bent it. Whoever it was
who drove the nail and stopped had tried
to be precise and notably failed
and left the failure there to see.
After considering this I still
oppose perfection or reaching it
and still believe in trying to—
that is what I meant by strange,
that is why I'm leaving the nail where it is
as if I'd driven it myself.

Red Bird, Black Sky

As any idea that suddenly
arrives, the one I've now divined
from simply looking up at a slight
angle affirms its plain importance.
The revelation itself reveals—
so the contrast between the red thing
and the black rings with clarity
like a note, a middle tone in the air,
and the air is its own reality
for the moment it takes the starkly red
and slashing bird to fly across it,
opening what briefly looks
like a wound but just as soon, as some
I've known, it's either sealed or gone.

The Tabernacle of Love

There was a church that called itself
The Tabernacle of Love. I stood
outside it once to hear the singing.
There was a lot of unison.
But a couple of voices were louder than
the others, and either above or below
by half a step, the note. A third
called out the verses in a kind
of hastened chant. It wasn't much
of a tabernacle, the windows were plain
and the light that entered them went straight
and uncolored into the room. I stood
outside and listened. The preacher, when
the singing wore down and ceased, sounded
unpolished—there was a wavering
in his voice—but I can tell you one thing
I've thought about. Some people I know
who are perfectly intelligent
would find this too emotional.
They're not the kind to be engaged
in this sort of thing, and I can see
it isn't ever lasting glory
that's going on in there, and no one
is going to be illuminated.
It isn't going to change the world,
these people standing around singing,
some of them crying and whimpering
and some not knowing why they're there.

AMIT MAJMUDAR

Instructions to an Artisan

Into the rood wood, where the grain's current splits
around the stones of its knots, carve eyelashes and eyelids.
Dye the knots, too—indigo, ink-black, vermillion
irises. These will be his eyes, always open, willing
themselves not to close when dust rises or sweat falls,
eyes witnessing, dimly, the eclipse that shawls
the shuddering hill, Jerusalem's naked shoulder.
The body itself? From a wick that still whiffs of smolder,
wax, because wax sloughs a smooth skein on the fingers just
below sensation's threshold. Prop the cross
upright and let the tear-hot wax trickle, slow, clot, taper
into a torso, thighs, calves, feet. Of Gideon Bible paper,
thinner than skin, cut him his scrap of cloth; embed
iron shavings in his forehead,
and, as the wax cools, scrape the rust off an old fuel can
to salt the whole wound that is the man.
Cry, if you feel like crying, and if no one else is there.
Then set it on the counter with your other wares.

Prayer

Lord, late though I am, slide the lathe
And shape, shave me. Shear me wraith-
Slim, slave-thin; flay the skin in moth-
Wings off my soul's loathed sheath. Wrath-
Ripe as I am, pluck me, pulp me. Filth
That I am, bathe me. Faith,
Be water; Father, help me drown.
I cannot breathe until you force me down.

The Christ-Frost

After I had burned alive a spell, spellbound
by the burning that bound me, I saw
an Ice Cross rising down to me through sea-
blue sky. This Ice Cross was the eye's cross,
submerged for years in the eye's
aqueous humor, an iceberg crux cracked off the Pole
Star and splashed deep—all this time to the surface surging.
The burning melted off my skin like rime,
and the Cross's seed-crystal ferned forth
like wiper fluid flash-freezing on a windshield.
Christ-frost plated the daylight,
a fast-branching, brittle fractal
sealing the spaces inside itself. At last
I could see the pane that separated me
from the one beyond me—a tiptoeing
child left out in the cold, eyes cupped
and trying to see in, his breath fogging the glass.

Horse Apocalypse

Hrhm Shp, colt-culling,
Is what hoof lore calls it—
The choke-chain sound a roan coined
To describe the things he saw
Before the sniff weevils crept
Up his nostrils and chewed
His eyes at the hue-sweet root.

- • -

Mother mares scare foals
From folly-trots and foxglove
By telling them fury tales
Of muck stirrup-deep and shells
Shoveling Passchendaele
Onto Passchendaele,
The foal fallen with the boy.

- • -

One memory, common
To all breeds, spurs night mares
Sparking down the mute streets
Of their sleep, gas-blind
Witnesses scraping Krupp
Guns over the cobblestones,
Winged sparks breeding in the hay.

- • -

Having watched us box and ditch
Our dead, they thought our dead
Ate termite-runnels
In the black bark of the land
And pulled all horsefolk down
To join whatever dark cavalry
Thundered underground.

- • -

The burlap gas mask cupped
And strapped to the wet snout
Could be mistaken, when
The gas gong sounded
And the men grew fly-heads,
For a feed sack chock-
Full of red ants.

SANDRA MARCHETTI

Migration Theory

The womb a tent
lit from within, fluttering
golden on the wind.

I'm given to pregnancy
dreams again.

Sleeping, the world becomes round once more—
sleeping atop my midriff. Sleeping in
silence and veins and skin—a globe, a missive.

I'm told the child
is ghost; instead

the sleep is lifted into,
alight with curiosities
curling out from the hand.

Sleep. The light sheet ruffles within.
White moths in flight
lift from the body—the skin.

Never-Ending Birds

Soft bulbs of morpho blue,
tight light pruned to a circuit,
the swallows feather and vector the wind.

I plume to watch, freshed in the ground;
they ring the trees as their own
sweet planets. Continuous streaks,
the green-blue preens take flying lessons,

beam to the ground they are bound by,
like no flown thing. They bring
around the ground and bright as floods
in winter, flap the wind that takes them,

pushes them into its envelope. The swallows,
so close, beat; I let them scrim
my stance, twist neatly solar.

I swallow, lift at my chest where the freckles
crack, where the wet wings gleam. Swallows
sweep out to swing my heart up with the hawk
who circles the skirmish, weeps, and screams.

PAUL MARIANI

Hopkins in Ireland

—FOR THE JESUIT COMMUNITY AT BOSTON COLLEGE

Above the blue-bleak priest the bright-blue fisher hovers.
The priest notes the book upon the table, the lamp beside the book.
A towering Babel of papers still to grade, and that faraway look
as once more the mind begins to wander. Ah, to creep beneath the covers

of the belled bed beckoning across the room. He stops, recovers,
takes another sip of bitter tea, then winces as he takes another look
at the questions he has posed his students and the twists they took
to cover up their benighted sense of Latin. The fisher hovers

like a lit match closer to him. The windows have all been shut against
the damp black Dublin night. After all these years, his collar chokes
him still, in spite of which he wears it like some outmoded mark
of honor, remembering how his dear Ignatius must have sensed
the same landlocked frustrations. Again he lifts his pen. His strokes
lash out against the dragon din of error. The fisher incandesces in the dark.

Epitaph for the Journey

Miles Davis cradling his gleaming
trumpet, three black jazzmen slouched
like hipster guardian angels just
behind him. Searing coals those eyes,

as they stare out from the photo at you.
The jagged blue-black mosaic shards
of Justinian's eyes under the golden
dome of San Appollinare, unblinking there

these fifteen hundred years. Listen long
enough, and you will hear the arpeggios
those eyes attend to. Hart Crane, doomed
pilgrim that he was, surely must have heard

them. At least his songs report back
that he did, descending from the giant harp
he called the Bridge. Lorca heard it too,
his dear dark lady, moonbright pupils facing

that blind unblinking firing squad. Father
Hopkins refused our four-bar player piano
measures, listening hard instead for the strain
of plainchant groaning off the stones

of Delphi, an ancient music flaking down
the Dead Sea cells of Qumran monks, or Monte
Cassino's choir stalls, before it disappeared
into the vast insolid Void. Others too,

they say, have heard it in the timeless
vortices of time. And now, if they have
anything at all to tell me, it is this:
my time, like yours, friend, is drawing

to a close, my one ear dead since birth,
the other closing down that much more
each month. Most go about their business
day by day. They keep their heads down

or learn to simply wait. Here and there
someone points or gestures here or there.
Unheard melodies, Keats called them, eyes
ablaze, then dimming as his body fell apart.

Once my own eyes blazed, but that was then.
Too late, someone else is singing. Too late.
But the high flung bells—if anyone can or cares
to hear them—keep choiring in the haunted risen wind.

CHRISTOPHER MARTIN

Parable of the Red-Tailed Hawks

The preachers may say they believe
in angels in all their glory—
whose glory comes filtered of God—
and say they hear their holy songs above,
imagine wings of light and silver,
feathers of white unflawed.

And that is well and good:

But I wonder how one can speak of angels,
whose wings we have not seen,
when red-tailed hawks fly over interstates
on black-dappled, rust, red, white-brushed,
creation-colored wings,

and nest on rooftops
angels never would.

MARIANA MCDONALD

Scoop

—FOR MIGUEL

Tapas and drinks with Miguel Algarín
in a shadowed spot off North. Waiters
twirled about, foodie dervishes.

Conversation flowed a Mississippi,
a Nile, a Seine, and when cheese
that piqued the tongue was gone,

we ordered sweets—a pear tart
sculpture served with ice cream,
a single dappled scoop.

I thought then of Gerard, how he'd
sing the praises of this dish,
this canvas of spottedness,

kin to wing, horse, sparrow's egg.
He saw in dull disorderedness
a sign of greatest order,

would have let the sugary cold
slide in his mouth
as joy kneeled on his tongue.

ASHLEY ANNA MCHUGH

What to Tell the Girl

—FOR SOPHIA

Sophia lifts the leaves above her head,
then lets them fall to earth a second time.
She knows, but is not sorry they are dead.
Far away, the silver church bells chime,

even though it's Tuesday afternoon,
for mourners. But her laughter is a charm
against the haunted mind, the daylight moon
looming in the sky. She means no harm,

so when she asks if I could bury her,
I can't say no. I build the pile high,
then under all those quiet leaves, I hear
a staggering breath as she begins to cry.

I whisk her out. *It was so dark inside*
all the colors, and I couldn't see—.
What to tell the girl? I can't decide,
and so I simply hold her close to me.

But now I realize what I should have told her:
Darkness is the least we have to fear,
and soon, Sophia, as your heart grows older,
as autumn leads to winter, year to year,

when empty branches whinny and crash, when wind
wails hard against the houses, cold and violent,
hurling the leaves in helpless arcs—you'll find
your mother's reflection in the window, silent,

and before your eyes, the dark will close again,
on you alone. You'll want to reminisce,
but as the windows rattle with the train,
you won't know what to think of.
                              So think of this:

How even as you cried, you were lifted out,
and how the weight above you was so light—
how even though your whimper wasn't loud,
I heard you; how the leaves were still so bright,

even though they seemed so dark to you—
and remember how you left my arms to play,
how soon you forgot your fear, as children do.
Then lift the leaves, and let them fall away.

LUCIEN DARJEUN MEADOWS

Finding Home by Taste, by Fire

Monongalia mountains rub their shoulders blue
With horizon, these hills dreaming themselves sky.
Hardwood forest by the highway, woodblanket

For hills scalped on the other side. I descend
From ridge to hollow, feel his coal in my pocket

Shake off the matte, oil itself glossy, hot. My leg
Glows red as the spray of cardinal flowers
Goat-high on a furred stalk, exhaling scarlet:

I breathe them in, loose a flight of bees
From each pore of my face, winging back

To drink each bright bell. As the trail rises again,
My ears vibrate with the drone of mosquitoes,
Machinery—a hum that still tells my body

It is summer, and your father may never come home.

Winter Solstice

after three weeks of snow   even morning folds
this hollow between mountains   in lengthening shadow
but when you follow me   back to our snowquilted bed
the yew beside us   bends a furred branch
to our window   lowers a cardinal
who spreads an exaltation of red   feather and wing

as we fall into thick drifts   each olive cone
swings on yewstem   when the cardinal trills
as if today   day of most darkness
each cone could disclose   nested red lips
these latent arils   open seedcups
a multitude of mouths   tongues tumbling toward river

and the cardinal tilts head   flutter and wing
yew branch waves   a beacon
a flame as I follow   the bright limbs of you
spiral through cloud and snow   out from our center
our horizon beginning   even now
to remember   the thrill of light

PHILIP METRES

Compline

That we await a blessed hope, & that we will be struck
With great fear, like a baby taken into the night, that every boot,

Every improvised explosive, Talon & Hornet, Molotov
& rubber-coated bullet, every unexploded cluster bomblet,

Every Kevlar & suicide vest & unpiloted drone raining fire
On wedding parties will be burned as fuel in the dark season.

That we will learn the awful hunger of God, the nerve-fraying
Cry of God, the curdy vomit of God, the soiled swaddle of God,

The constant wakefulness of God, alongside the sweet scalp
Of God, the contented murmur of God, the limb-twitched dream-

Reaching of God. We're dizzy in every departure, limb-lost.
We cannot sleep in the wake of God, & God will not sleep

The infant dream for long. We lift the blinds, look out into ink
For light. My God, my God, open the spine binding our sight.

Elegy for D.S.

ISAIAH 40, 1-5

Until the day falls there is nothing
I can say, my friend. Until
the mountain kneels. He suffered
so long in wordless suffering, a pain

without wounds. May your brother,
who belongs now to remember,
be restored to light as wood is
by ember. Whatever relief it brings.

Restore him, Unthinkable, before
the voices roiled his head. Before windshield genuflected before
his trouble-lovely face. Before night

broke like a window, & blackness
spread. Unspeakable, restore us,
we who belong to nothing
that will not cease, to nothing

that will. Until the day falls,
my friend, nothing I can say
that will bring this dark to heel.
Until the mountain kneels.

SUSAN LAUGHTER MEYERS

Praise Song for Nikky Finney

THIS, ALL THIS BEAUTY BLOOMING.
—*Gerard Manley Hopkins*

She goes hatless, which is not to say
she wrongs God, which is not to say
she doesn't cover her head in His house.
Her hair is her hat, ribbons of braids.
If every hat has its occasion, she wears hers—
no feather, no floribunda rose—for liberty's sake.
Consider the braids, thick brown arguments
flowing halfway down her back,

how they weave in and out among themselves,
how they mimic her voice, warm and going somewhere
with truth-ticking cadence. The riddle of her hair
and riddle of her tongue compose a sonnet
whose subject is love, that common necessity.
Those bold, bountiful arguments: praise them.

Coastland

When the wind gets up and the water rises,
those who live on higher ground, at a distance
from the pinched smell of pluff mud,
from spartina marshes and swamps of cypress knees,
upland from the tannin-black tributaries
where through the bottoms, among the wet-footed
spider lilies, one barred owl
calls another, one to the other till there's little left to say,
upland from the cottonmouth and the brown water snake
coiled and rooted by the tupelo
and the alligators logging across the slough,
upland from the deer hound pens full of yelps—
full of naps and pacing, full of cedar-thicket dreaming—
and the dirt yard's milling of gray cats
and striped kittens yawning by the palmettos,
upland from the sea sky sea—the horizon
a fine line polished away—
from the shrimp boats shrinking smaller and smaller
on their way to their serious work of gathering,
from the smooth, quick balancing act
of the sun—heavy and orange—riding the waves,
upland from salt myrtle and the season's second growth
of trumpet honeysuckle, those who live at a distance
from the band of quick, dark clouds blooming at sea,
upland from the bang and whirl, clatter
and shake of the wind when it's up,
those who live on higher ground ask
of those who live by the flats and shoals,
the shallows and bogs, *Why*, and again, *Why, O why.*

MAREN O. MITCHELL

Breath and Bread

A FOUND POEM BASED ON "THE WRECK OF THE *DEUTSCHLAND*"

Bound bones and veins, I did say yes.
Down with a horror, laced with fire!
You were dovewinged, to flash
from the flame to the flame.
I am soft, but steady as water in a well,
since mystery must be stressed. I greet
days, not out of bliss, but in dense sweat—
hard. Mouthed? Never ask:
wring malice, tongue love.

Stealing mercy, some rail and dream.
Flesh within sight, forget the sour,
tell souls the blessing of the sky, the sea, deeps to ride.
Carved with cares, hope shone and shook, stirred to save.
God's cold night roared, touched bone, mother of heart.

The rash call of the storm's brawling, beast of the dawn,
sucked love, light, sight. The word, time-taken, at rest.
Comfort hovers: jay-blue height, moth-soft Milky Way, tenderer.
Apart, measure sight, look at it.
The extremity, living and dead, triumph, doom:
single eye!

Present and past, blast light without stain!
Pity the comfortless,
tides fall and recurb—death hides.
The listener glides the vein, the last mark.
Not dazzle nor dark, but reclaiming lightning at our door.
Remember, reign rolls pride, hearts fire thoughts.

MEREDITH MOENCH

I Waked and Fell

About the end, nothing said says right.
Words weigh, bricks upon backs, bruise, but weight
Stays. Weary and wonderwhelmed, full-fledged in wait,
Flailing, failing, we fall graceless into night.

Weeks, weak, we try to keep days in sight,
sand sifting between a finger grate.
And fear, free-reign fears, negate
Our sleep, and fresh feed worries alas! daylight

A tree falls, thuds deadly deaf
ening hush, then nothing. But leaf
Remnants down. Which fall, fell I? Felled

By saws, diplomas, fluttered by Christ's breath
To dank floor flushed in leaves' death,
Feeling fully we are selving; but undwelled.

ROBERT MORGAN

Maple Gall

What looks at first like rotten fruit,
hung round the maple's slender trunk,
we know's a tortured cluster of
malignancies where cells grow drunk
with larvae, mites, or fungus, worms,
with virus or bacteria,
and multiply as tumors, bulge
of goiters, awful excess growths.
But when you look at all the gross
disfigurements at closer range
you see the beauty of distortion,
the sculpture of disease, the strange
and replicating work the tree
is not supposed to yield, a flowery
production so grotesque it seems
a kind of miracle in wood
that makes this sapling both unique
and memorable by virtue of
its suffering swollen sores and scars,
the warts that are its finest art.

Algae

The stuff in ditches early spring
could be a luminous refuse,
the lumps and clots, the dumplings green
and golden, just the muck of life
in hairy chunks of phosphorescence.
It multiplies as mulch around
the roots of cattails, ferns and reeds,
and thickens to a luscious paste
of photosynthetic essence
of tiny vegetables at base
of a gigantic food chain maze.
And floating free in slimy whirls
it shoulders up the living world.

Aspen Song

The sound of water in the air
cools even summer sunlight,
as though the upland pasture
remembers oceans at this height
when even dirt and rocks were young
(warm-bloodied life had just begun).
The breeze plays leaves in sweetest treble
and never tires of its long fable,
in counterpoint to human foible.

Left Behind

When half the mighty willow fell,
broke off and crashed into the field,
it seemed ironic that it was
the living half the wind struck down.
The side left standing was all dead,
a skeleton of scaling bark
with pecker holes like marks of war.
You'd think the living half would be
the part most likely to survive.
The dead side might have crumbled long
ago. But living leaves resist
the wind and bear the brunt and lash
and tangle with the storm and take
the punishment to hold their foils
against an angry hurricane.
And now both sides are dead except
the longer dead still stands, goes on
for years perhaps, so lean, alone.

ANGELA ALAIMO O'DONNELL

Hawk in the Bronx

"I caught this morning morning's minion."
—*Gerard Manley Hopkins*

Perched on a church
scolding stone

Hawkeye owns
his daily glory.

He wives the wind
and chides the world

whose children make
their earthward way

asleep beneath the wing
of their unknowing.

Being pure bird,
minor miracle of air,

he is stranger to despair,
the ordinary agony

that halves the merely
human heart.

The easy feast he devours
each of every bell-knelled hour

escapes those who live too low.
Twice-blessed is he to know

the saint's sweet rapture
impossible to capture.

MELISSA RANGE

The Canary

This miner's minion,
　　this drab rendition of light
yellow, feathers faded, slated
saffron—weatherbeaten
　　(as if there were weather here):

the canary, pitched
　　past pitch of countermelody,
chirrs its cagey call to the tune
of coal, the pickaxes
　　steeling themselves for the sharp,

the flat, the odd strike
　　of luck or a skittish match.
Tapping a channel with hammers,
the miners trail by threads
　　of song slanting through caverns,

shrill as a drillbit
　　scarping the rock to carbon.
But mountains shift their pilings, shafts
of rockdust hovering
　　in hacked-out pockets, in lungs,

between the feeble
　　warblings of a canary
harrowed to slag. When the air cracks,
the string snaps, the return
　　blurs—it's the foretold collapse,

core to conduits:
　　the blackdamp, the igneous
blast, the bird guttered from its perch,
the labyrinth tautly laced
　　onto a shuttle. Little

birds, broods bred for dank
    and death, for lost myths—the maze
hot in the throat, the notes a pyre—
what beast of sacrifice
cannot guess its saving fire?

Christ Imagined as Cavalry Commander

Chevalier, your soldiers aren't so sure
of your command: you told them
that you came to bring a sword;
when they draw theirs, you holler reprimands.

You can't settle on an enemy:
to you, the uniforms all look the same,
bachelor-patched, stitched scattershot
when there are any scraps and any thread.

Although you speak of every skirmish
like it might be your last stand, your recruits
grow restless waiting for the charge;
while you sleep, they raise alarums in your name.

Incensed, you wrench the sabers and the carbines
from their fists, then hatchet the limbers,
slap the pack and cannon horses free.
Wondering why they bothered to enlist,

your troops disband, leaving you alone,
afield, with nothing but their surplus gear,
their cookfires snuffed and smudged into the mud,
and their galloping adversaries, whose flesh

is grass. You love the grass, and every nail
in every hoof that rips it from the earth,
in which you sink your sword, smiling at your coup,
your last and best-laid stratagem.

You've lost, once and for all. That pleases you.

October Trees

I can no longer think of you in vague groves;
I can no longer think of you without proper names—

and not just tulip-poplar, one standing among many,
but *this* tulip-poplar, this windy one scouring my screen:

you, brokenfingered fire-eater, tallest-in-the-yard,
arrow of God or of something else, quick alchemist:

you will be called Goldreen, and you will outpace
the almanacs with your turnings, and if you fall too fast,

I can but watch. Only you can fathom the source
of your secret name, and only you can beat out the song

of harps hung from your light-strangled branches.
And the names of those who might've played them.

I must quit my day job. I have found another calling:
to expose the lie of the foreign tongue, the notion

of human understanding—that I should not listen
to bark or bray or cool flutter, that I should not dog-ear

the unpaged dictionaries waving in every trunk,
that I should not learn a dirge for the *each* of you,

rather than the all, for in the all is nothing
either of us can keep. Sawfallen, Splitlightning,

Allorange, Ovenflame, Slightring, Coldpenny,
Leatherlantern—how will I have time to sleep?

Prayer to the Birds

Mockingbird, tanager, thrush—you liltwings,
you hopscotch-skippers—forgive us our calling,

noun-bound to be proper, to freight
your pinions with what yokes our weight

to gravity, law, numbers, other fables.
Forgive us our starry quills, our parables—

rook, raven, crow, canary, dove—
our willful migration from love

to symbol. Wind-sickles, forgive us the sins
visited on Icarus, his fathers and sons:

our conceit in zeppelin and satellite, the feast
of false hawks, false eagles. Forgive us as priests

in slums and picket lines forgive the church:
in vigilance, mining the breach—

that sky—for something that will not be owned.
Cardinal, finch—forgive us our lone

hiding behind bushes, spying you out
when we should be flying at your side, not

from pride but from humility: that soaring
force that finds its power in adoring.

RON RASH

Dylan Thomas

Scrawmy, gray-souled November
blinds the whale-road, pall draper
over this ship bearing one
whose name means *of the ocean*
in a language he denied
allegiance to, though his lines
rang with cynghanedd—English
reined in by Celtic music,
stitched tight as the oracle
that wombed Taliesin—tribal
rain-downs of sound, not enough:
a small people lose their tongue
one poet at a time. Talent-
squanderer, fraud, miscreant,
apt sobriquets for a life
lived badly between the lines.
The coast recedes. Last gulls cry.
Down in the hold his drunk wife
smokes and flirts with the seamen
who play cards on his coffin.

The Corpse Bird

Bed-sick she heard the bird's call
fall soft as a pall that night
quilts tightened around her throat,
her gray eyes narrowed, their light
gone as she saw what she'd heard
waiting for her in the tree
cut down at daybreak by kin
to make the coffin, bury
that perch around her so death
might find one less place of rest.

Speckled Trout

Water-flesh gleamed like mica:
orange fins, red flankspots, a char
shy as ginseng, found only
in spring-flow gaps, the thin clear
of faraway creeks no map
could name. My cousin showed me
those hidden places. I loved
how we found them, the way we
followed no trail, just stream-sound
tangled in rhododendron,
to where slow water opened
a hole to slip a line in,
and lift as from a well bright
shadows of another world,
held in my hand, their color
already starting to fade.

Fall Creek

As though shedding an old skin,
Fall Creek slips free from fall's weight,
clots of leaves blackening snags,
back of pool where years ago
local lore claims clothes were shed
by a man and woman wed
less than a month, who let hoe
and plow handle slip from hands,
left rows half done, crossed dark waves
of bottomland to lie on
a bed of ferns, make a child,
and all the while the woman
stretching both arms behind her
over the bank, hands swaying
wrist-deep in current—perhaps
some old wives' tale, water's pulse
pulsing what seed might be sown,
or just her need to let go
the world awhile, let the creek
wash away every burden
her life had carried so far,
open a room for this new
becoming as her body
flowed around her man like water.

JANEEN PERGRIN RASTALL

Fossil Hunting at the Quarry

—AFTER GERARD MANLEY HOPKINS

Leaves slick our boot bottoms,
you grab my hand. I clutch
a sack. We wind down
the rock cut where
gypsum was pried
from the sediment. We search
for fern fronds impressed
in the chert. Our eyes intent
on patterns
in variegated stone,
we never see
the breeze unleaf the birch tree,
gold tumble
to the quarry's heart,
a leaf filigree sink below.

JOSHUA ROBBINS

Equinoctial

Nearly October and the front oak's branches
    are mostly quicksilvered,

though we watch
    a handful here, a handful there

of leaves tinge copper.
    Beneath the zodiac's turning wheels

and the stars' nocturnal parade,
    the moon, pockmarked and mottled,

stamps night's scroll,
    and luminescent sealing wax

drips through leaf-lattice,
    puddles around our feet.

Caught in the celestial tilt-and-balance,
    we wear our brief freedom

like constellational moneychangers,
    all glitz and glimmer,

and weigh the disks of sun and moon
    like two coins on the pans of Libra's scales.

That is how it mostly goes.
    Blindly, we rummage around for an evener:

the black wick inside the candle's flame,
    our fingertips licked.

A Question of Ear

One by one, the street lamps' sodium-purr clicks off
   as my neighbor's half-ton coughs
      and revs, coughs, and finally turns over

and he heads off, a gravel tire-churn
   as a gangsta rap bassline thumps from the cab,
      circles out like pond water

after a stone's plunk. "In the end it's all
   a question of ear," says Kierkegaard, meaning the *next* life:
      the next life as pure music, heaven's harmonic

resolve of Being's sour arpeggio. But for now,
   suburbia is tuned to dream's white noise,
      that octave three steps above wakefulness,

the one right before the clock radio
   bleeps on and the percolator auto-grinds,
      and the front door rehearses its slam.

The Mercy Seat

Crepuscule rain ricochet,
Desk genesis-insipid summed and pale blue-rinsed,
Floor cloud-break quadrangled and daylight paged.
It's a teasing,
                these words and their maneuverings
Blacked on white and smudged and swapped,
Models ribbing models ribbing models,
Their lures, allusive and flicked, this sacrament sought
And never
                is it not caught, its metaphors
Like invisible hooks in my lips
Lined to the body of what I cannot see,
The ink on the shadowless source-side.
Metaphysician and skeptic,
                                faith unfaithed,
Mine's both the cloak hood's cowled want
And the sleeping hand's inner hush.
I'm talking about wish and suspicion,
The prayer of the page unblanked
                                versus the of,
Both bridge and barrier.
Failure into wonder, that's the task.
Synapse-spark and pleasure-doubt.
One must conceal
                to reveal.
Ascent is as often smoke as it is ascent
And doubt like a burning glass.
As often as fire we become the stars.

DON SHARE

Savior

What would a Savior make of our half-thoughts?
He is busy with the skirt of rain,
the bric-a-brac lands birds flee from,
the zoning sun. Before redeeming any more
of the landscape, He would know its true color,
and who sees it. Savior? Means taste.

- • -

Surely He would know
we have capitulated
in every way.

- • -

Even the best blood
pools in beds
under an equator of slaughter.

- • -

God makes only geniuses,
but our idiom grows crooked, its marrow
a broken skeleton's. Yet
till the air becomes air again,
there is always something that can be learned,
even in the awful grates of death.

- • -

If the salt
hath lost its savour
wherewith
shall it be salted?

- • -

Where is the so-called fat of the land?
The thick branches respond
to rain
in jeweled form.
Hence, leaves.
Hence, bees keen on the blossom,
blackbirds drawn from the life.
Round May
the land gorges,
while the crow is always starved.

- • -

Earth totters,
lifts up its horn to the heavens,
while its inhabitants grow yet
rich and poor together
and speak with insolent neck.

DEREK SHEFFIELD

Ornithology 101

Now that you have staked their skeletons,
eyed the scope of a throat, prodded
strutted white ribs, pinched
a wishbone for resilience, thumbed
a keeled sternum's edge still trying
to steer scattered feathers, stroked
a hummingbird's mum iridescence, ruffed
the white down of a great egret
slit and stuffed as last year's final project,
sprinted with a severed wing to catch
the physics, given new vision
to a blackbird with two dabs of cotton,
you can leave with an *A* in class *Aves*.
Now that you have looked through birds, you see
the diagrammatic movements of geese
across the blue sky, dotted lines
narrowing a million years. You expect
from every American goldfinch thistles
and sadness, and when you walk out
among the world's perches and Latinate streaks
at the edge of sight, the air is feathers
measuring the bones of your face.

Oystermen

What comfort to see them trudge on the tideland
back and forth with nets and buckets,
dredging for puddles of ripened, lung-shaped oysters.
Bundles of thick coats and boots, they plant lanterns
and hunker in small glows to pick
secret after knobby, clicking secret.

Lowest tides draw them late night down
the bank of surf grass, crunching across sand dollars
and crab shells, clattering from the rocks
and slurching to their muddy bed while I slip
into mine. With slowing eyes, I watch them roam
and dazzle like prehistoric fireflies,

call out over the blue-green mussel worm
that twists a slimed gleam in the muck,
the severed arm of the six-rayed star,
some kind of eye globbed on a stick. The one
with the roughest hands keeps to himself
until a dying fire coaxes him open for the children.

I wake before dawn and they are there,
gathered breath steaming as they spangle
the wet emptiness and clump in mud-heavied boots.
At every bright lump shucked
out of the dark by a joggled lantern,

I want to surge down and labor shoulder
to shoulder, grab the ridged, slippery shells
in my pale hands, break each gritty fruit
from its cluster and become something other
than their midden ghosting the shore,
the relinquishing moon of jellyfish—to do
a work of weight, of being
one of the shades among the lights
before the cold sea climbs my legs.

Prayer with Fur

Down a scarp of gray rock and dust,
    not a brook, not even
        a rill, but a lick
dribbles, through sheer heat,
    all day and under every flood
        night ends. Mud the color of dusk
remembers an earlier slither,
    and skinned roots claw
        a coolness in air

flowing past my shins. I kneel
    and call Ginger to the water
        in my a hands, a cold shock,
a splash of the first night
    out of the Garden,
        two people on their backs
under the unlocked stars,
    touching along arms and legs,
        silenced by a glittering distance.

Here, on the trail to Temple Ridge,
    my dog lowers her face, looks to mine,
        and laps, and keeps lapping
until my hands are open and empty
    but for stroke after stroke
        of her insistent tongue.

Prayer with Game

As far as you can see are seabirds
    that won't stop dying, won't stop
making a froth-slicked slag heap

of this beach, this riot of wings
    restless as rats. You can't help
but watch them peck and scrabble

across sand and rock, every species
    beyond the reach of wave
after wave of shushing in—and that anemic C

of moon that looks to be floating
    just above their flocked panic.
Bloom is no name for *this*, these splashes

of red feathers, of loons lying
    in white collars like clergy
fresh from a stabbing. They won't stop

crying, shrill infants left to the elements,
    cry after rising cry
until you pray for joystick and screen,

a chance to plug in and propel
    your radiant self beyond this level.
Instead of phytoplankton, gigabytes

and a fair fight in which you could bring it,
    breeze over waves and click
each ruby icon of each loon eye and win.

MARK SMITH-SOTO

Collateral Damage

"Workers at a state-of-the-art solar plant in the Mojave Desert have a name for birds that fly through the plant's concentrated sun rays—'streamers,' for the smoke plume that comes from birds that ignite in midair" —*Christian Science Monitor*

I caught this morning, mourning, sight
of you who flew into sky
you thought your own

and caught the sun down
to the marrow bones, tender embers
scorched there, sputter-guttered there,

your far-flung flair undone mid-air,
tailspin, trailspin of plummeting
ash—

oh, flame on, you seared ones,
dear ones, take us by the heart,

let your blackened, blown feathers
fan our rage, outrage us,
engage

our careworn, too careless, caring.

CHERYL STILES

These Fatals

"DEATH BLOTS BLACK OUT..."
—*Gerard Manley Hopkins*

A bubble in a mine's vein meets
spark, flash. A blast of heat
breaks shafts, rains dust—black,
wild widow-making, a wreck.
Profiteers offer more PR,
no problem until *these fatals this year.*
Near the coast of New Orleans
a platform blows. Flatscreens,
phones fill—damage control,
more dark suits hailing
dark gods, Coal and Petrol.
And a top kill failing—
debris, dust, more plumes of oil—
marsh-bound, gulf-bound jinn turning.

Elemental

"LEAVE COMFORT ROOT-ROOM..."
—*Gerard Manley Hopkins*

Comfort me, can you, at Betty's creek near Beech Trail's edge? Herb gatherer, manroot,
mandrake man, make of the auburn strands of my hair kindling, a coiled tinder. With flint,
single flick

of wrist, start and tend a fire. Off! To the great horned owl's lament, slip off
this cobalt-colored dress. With it winnow the flames higher. Blue dress—blue center of flame.

Incense of oakstem and leafmold, smoke from roots—you incant their Linnaean names.
Heat everywhere, outside and within, rises—rill of blood and desire—rises like ladder rungs.

Herb gatherer, manroot, mandrake man, do you love this burning?
Comfort me. You can. Savor salt, sweat, skin. Taste the ashes on your tongue.

MARY SZYBIST

Via Negativa

Sometimes it's too hard with words or dark or silence.
Tonight I want a prayer of high-rouged cheekbones
and light: a litany of back-lit figures,
lithe and slim, draped in fabrics soft and wrinkleless and pale
as onion slivers. Figures that won't stumble or cough:
sleek kid-glove Astaires who'll lift
ladies with glamorous sweeps in their hair—
They'll bubble and glitter like champagne.
They'll whisper and lean and waltz and wink effortlessly
as figurines twirling in music boxes, as skaters in their dreams.

And the prayer will not be crowded.
You'll hear each click of staccato heel
echo through the glossy ballrooms—too few shimmering skirts;
the prayer will seem to ache
for more. But the prayer will not ache.
When we enter, its chandeliers and skies
will blush with pleasure. Inside
we will be weightless, and the goodness will not matter
in a prayer so light, so empty it will float.

In Tennessee I Found a Firefly

Flashing in the grass; the mouth of a spider clung
    to the dark of it: the legs of the spider
held the tucked wings close,
    held the abdomen still in the midst of calling
with thrusts of phosphorescent light—

When I am tired of being human, I try to remember
    the two stuck together like burrs. I try to place them
central in my mind where everything else must
    surround them, must see the burr and the barb of them.
There is courtship, and there is hunger. I suppose
    there are grips from which even angels cannot fly.
Even imagined ones. *Luciferin, luciferase.*
    When I am tired of only touching,
I have my mouth to try to tell you
    what, in your arms, is not erased.

Knocking or Nothing

Knock me or nothing, the things of this world
ring in me, shrill-gorged and shrewish,

clicking their charms and their chains and their spouts.
Let them. Let the fans whirr.

All the similar virgins must have emptied
their flimsy pockets, and I

was empty enough,
sugared and stretched on the unmown lawn,

dumb as the frost-pink tongues
of the unpruned roses.

When you put your arms around me in that moment,
when you pulled me to you and leaned

back, when you lifted me
just a few inches, when you shook me

hard then, had you ever heard
such emptiness?

I had room for every girl's locket,
every last dime and pocketknife.

Oh my out-sung, fierce, unthinkable—
why rattle only the world

you placed in me? Won't you clutter the unkissed,
idiot stars? They blink and blink

like quiet shepherds,
like brides-about-your-neck.

Call them out of that quietness.
Knock them in their nothing, against their empty enamel,

against the dark that has no way to hold them
and no appetite.

Call in the dead to touch them.
Let them slip on their own chinks of light.

R. K. R. THORNTON

Gerard Manley Hopkins (1844–1889)

FROM *ADLESTROPHES*, RE-ENVISIONINGS OF EDWARD THOMAS'S
'ADLESTROP' IN THE STYLE OF OTHER POETS

I caught that noontide nothing but the name
Of Adlestrop, where stopped the non-stop train
At the year's centre, sent my scenting brain
No trace or clue that memory can reclaim.

Engine and man did one thing and the same,
Hissed mist from out their pipes, but how explain
How stationary the station could remain
To lay stress on the sign? For that I came.

Codlins and cream, green grass, and all the willows,
Sweet meadowsweet, hay dry beneath sun's fires,
Clouds echoing stooks below like silk-sack pillows,
Made hush while blackbird's song set off the choirs
That cry their maker forth, from hill to hill, O,
Shout wide to Oxford and its sharing shires.

PIMONE TRIPLETT

A Local Landfill's Invitation to Trash Left on the Moon

Come, moon-man, luna leaper,
settle that orbit up,
season-ease yourself. I'm wild

to be whiffed. Each rose a brick
laid down all delilah. Each
dumpy tonnage of me, I admit,

is reeky wreck, some cat food sauté
with chlorox deglazed.
Forgive me, or them, whichever

the case may be. Or come sit beside
my cattail's thrashy sways.
Bathe and be, joliesse a la pond,

unsomber in summer, can't let
a few rats phase us. Get here,
old pal, hiding your fat in

hug wraps, yield more at
my burning barrel. Let flame tips
gust sense and its non

from us, to sire, beget, congest us
by shine or ash, this trash, compost
cuddled up at a weigh station. Or

else keep me, dear ditto,
sky-scuttler, till at last all
that utters is atlas, arriving anon.

Oil

Excuse me if I'm crude—
    who loses in who's who? I get
the axis of evil all
    slicked up. Catch me if you can
or pop the can open cause
    my Esso, my Exxon, my Ex
says tubs of me rev you up
    better and better. One embargo's
largesse drillbits the next.
    Baby, find me,
refine me, rewind me.
    Trade autocrats
for crapper's rats.
    Someone's always got the cash
but who said the guy behind
    the counter's got the keys?
I can burn the midnight.
    Don't dissolve.
Betcha insight's
    industrial, thicker than,
quicker than.
    Alas, dictates lubricate
a better rate, yes?
    Give me the grease monkeys,
call me texas tea. Without me,
    try jump starting
your neighbor's Hummer
    cold mornings.
Sure, I flirt with records,
    posh dollars, more.
But I feel sorry for some
    of my suitors, the losers
over my barrel, so many
    accident-prone. And what about
the other ancient fossils,
    fueled less rare, about whom
who cares? Ah, deposits keep
    the whatsits running, drip, drip,
so petrol's just a love-in.
    These blacktops on fire, vroom.

Ego

Be clear as a glass house
ladled in plates, liquid
silica, sand, dolomite, lime,

then tempered, shaped, craned
till you stand fastened
to forest floor, reflecting.

Let the sudden garden strut
up, rising in ribboned slope,
pine and pin oak, laurel,

fleabane, draw markers for
their names, it's all yours, the bits
of talisman and tame.

Also, quit that stupid trembling.
You could be the wild
turkey last season who slammed

the glass again and again, all
gobble and snood, scrimmage
of spit, wattles on fire at first

seeing itself. Be the crash
that comes after crack.
Else, you're nothing but the single

shard that hangs for its moment,
see-through guillotine,
over the broken world.

DAMIAN WALFORD DAVIES

THREE POEMS FROM *DOCKLANDS*

Perspective

From this gothic bay, flung out
above the cab stand

where O'Driscoll's pony
rests a ruined fetlock

on a backturned hoof,
I can see St Mary Street run plumb

until, a quarter-mile away,
it curves to kiss itself

beyond the French arcades.
I lead each client to this

balanced brink; instinctively,
he backs away. Revelation-

thin, O'Driscoll's nag
evacuates the day in coarse, tan

gobs, heady sweetness
mixing with my new bay rum.

Spouse

Past ten, she has the desk lamp
in my study lit, *to lure me*

like a moth, she taunted,
home. Through the saplings

of Sophia Gardens, I see
the light prick darkness

like a spiteful eye.
She meets me on the landing

still in black—gaunt hand
resting on the newel post's

carved artichoke. Did I not also hold
the stillbirth in my palm

before they wrapped it in a pall
no bigger than my handkerchief?

I loathe her pallor, hate the acrid
odour when I douse the lamp.

Saw

I was in The Packet's parlour
with our dandy Clerk of Works,

toasting our foundation stone—
my name carved deep

in stark sans-serif. We were
on our fourth French brandy

when they lugged a docker
screaming through a side door

in a sail—his crushed and cockeyed
peg appalling. From nowhere,

someone set to work: knifestrokes,
sawstrokes, reef knot

to the artery, and the grey girl
watching from the far side

of the room, indifferent
as they let the waste leg go.

DANIEL WESTOVER

Breeze-Born

—for Eden at Easter

This afternoon, beneath a blue egg sky,
Eden sprints, her six year-old arms stretched
to catch a Frisbee's fall.

At the yard's edge, pears are brash
with blossoms. Plump bees sift
in purple stamens, hover in honeyed canopies.

Beneath this unlocked lattice, she, shade-striped,
gives chase, rescues and flings the Frisbee back
with elbow-whip and wrist.

With every toss, softened for small fingers,
I throw ghosts of seasons fallen, watch them float
from my father's callused hands.

And I am running with Eden to catch them, but the quick wind
shifts, and my toss, like my father's,
wings wild, tree-ward.

Impossible not to slip, to miss her. The disc
strikes a forked branch. Bees, blossoms
break scattershot, windwheeling.

Hard to say who chases now, who runs
from what rises. The graves have emptied.
Everything is breeze-born.

But she is here, too, laughing, circling back
to meet what is falling from the tree—
these petals, broken, blessed as any bread.

Margaret's Reply

> "Leaves, like the things of man, you
> With your fresh thoughts, care for, can you?"
>   —G. M. Hopkins

I can, sir, though you look surprised
that falling leaves have caught my eye.
Why should you stand there so amazed
the dying year could make me cry?

True, I am a child with a child's hands
and a child's eyes. But these have felt
the dying seed: the broken ends
of pods that shrink and leaves that wilt.

Inside this very grove, I found
a blackbird stiff and torn. Her breast
was ice. Above the darkened ground,
her eggs were frozen in the nest.

The gardener sets his traps beneath
these golden boughs. I've seen a fox
with a snapped leg, his finished breath
frosting a grave of rocks and sticks.

I think of these when summer dies
and leaves cry out in silent flame.
It may be true that when I'm wise
I'll call them by a different name.

But today, my ghost is not guessing.
The loss I feel is sharp and deep.
I can't know what the years will bring,
but sir, I *do* know why I weep.

KATHARINE WHITCOMB

Sea Journal

Meanwhile, I shucked my shelter. Meanwhile. Writes Hopkins *what you look at hard seems to look hard at you hence*…will it open? Hard enough will it change like that sky so fused, so soaked one can only, one need only lie down in it? As I did. Blue of swoons, blue bruise, great inkdark, fogdark bank of night. Elephantine blue-sheered night. Lost toppled moon on her back in blue, loose in her bearings, lost in something other than thought, other than mind, than dream. Blue enough to devour. Blue to oblivion.

SARAH ANN WINN

The Baker Falls for Hopkins

Glory be to God for appled things—
for counters stretched dusty with flour as dirt roads,
for plate palates green-gashed with red, doled,
for cut, peeled and portioned plenty, for strudel rings,
for spice cakes and sauces, for amber juice, for a la mode,
for cider, spiced and mulled, or cold.

All dumplings, starrified, crimped, arranged. Whatever is
oven-ready, brushed with egg yolks, overloaded
with orchards-full, caramelized, ripened to gold,
sugar-crusted, milk beads riding pillion. Memorialize.
        Bake them.

JOHN WOOD

A Sestina for Mishima

"THE SWEET DROP OF HONEY THAT WAS TIME"
—*Yukio Mishima*

Wheat, sun, honey, gold, light, amber: these are the words held in the amber of memory. They stir in dreams of wheat swaying in bright and attic light. They rustle on slow dialed days as the sun glories down like golden bees humming of honey, those days held in the honeycomb of life's bright amber, days of our making but out of a time of gold, when all is seen as abundant wheat, as sun and summer light. And we are like those bees lighting in time's honey, drinking the nectar of life's harvest, suddened into joy as the sun quickens in winter, as amber charges the touch, as wind-whipped wheat sweeps our sight, and gold sets our lusts in shimmered gold-flecked light falling on wheat, on the honeyed sheaves rising under an amber sun. And then when that sun glows like gold and electrumed amber, when it throbs with the light's rhythmed waves, who could refuse the dense, darkling honey of love, or loaves made from the thrusting wheat? Who could allow the sun's canticles or the choiring wheat eclipse? Not even age can debase such gold, for lost light always glows in the ambered hold of Time's honey.

Η Ποιητική

I dream of perfect forms,
Of poems like Parthenons,
A frieze of fluid words
So cut in Attic odes
    Clarity blazes out to shine
    And beauty—even in ruin.

Bare marble's windy frame
And gold Athene's ghost
Are all that now remain
To prove, or haunt, the loss
    Of intellect's purest moment
    And beauty's unadorned intent.

Those broken stones sing out
Brighter than any art
My pen or thought might craft
And make me try to carve
    The stone to find that shimmered sound,
    Those fluid folds of her marble gown.

WILLIAM KELLEY WOOLFITT

Meditation on the Hands of a Boy Miner

Nails split, he cups
his hands to his chest,
hides the seams that cross

his palms, scar-lines
of labors for his father,
chunks sorted, braces built.

He clenches his hands
like tree buds—never open,
always spring. The space

inside them, so near his heart,
must be holy—formless, empty,
dark as cave streams, sump

pools, the face of the waters
where the spirit broods
before it calls out the light.

The Acolyte

When he tugs the rope, the bell creaks.
Flakes of rust tumble down. Cobwebs
catch in his hair, and the empty nests
of swallows unravel, pelt the ground

with dirt-gobs and faded grass.
As he stoops to sift the nest-shreds,
his hand branches, speaks and spells
the surge of sap in his blood

to the coltsfoot and chervil that spring
out of the dirt when light pours
from the tipped crock of sky. He yanks
the rope again, the air around him splits,

and the bell pitches
back and forth. His bones ring,
and the bell spills a stream of words
from its loosed and quickened tongue.

Boy with Kite

Thirteen years old and bundled
against the chill, he pastes rags and papers
to a frame that's cockeyed, loose,
all droop and strange angles.

What the kite needs is a breeze to rise.
Sticks poking out, paper ripping,
it catches the smallest blown breath
like a dead leaf taking to flame,

and swings from his hands, swoops and glides.
He runs forward, unreels the spool.
Someday, he will go out, and instead of this wind
so cold it might be from heaven's iced dome,

he believes there will be a girl, freckled,
brunette, quick eyes and feet, warm as
the blue mittens on his hands, glad to run
alongside him, to fling puffball dust

at him in the ironweed fields,
and curl against him as he sleeps.
If he goes on running, it will
take him to a joy that breaks him.

He reels in the wind-torn kite
before it lifts him from his skin.

CHARLES WRIGHT

Jesuit Graves

Midsummer. Irish overcast. Oatmeal-colored sky.
The Jesuit pit. Last mass
For hundreds whose names are incised on the marble wall
Above the gravel and grassless dirt.
Just dirt and the small stones—
                    how strict, how self-effacing.

Not suited for you, however, Father Bird-of-Paradise,
Whose *plumage of far wonder* is not formless and not faceless,
Whatever you might have hoped for once.
Glasnevin Cemetery, Dublin, 3 July 1995.
For those who would rise to meet their work,
                    that work is scaffolding.

Sacrifice is the cause of ruin.
The absence of sacrifice is the cause of ruin.
Thus the legends instruct us,
North wind through the flat-leaved limbs of the sheltering trees,
Three desperate mounds in the small, square enclosure,
                    souls God-gulped and heaven-hidden.

P Gerardus Hopkins, 28 July 1844–8 June 1889, Age 44.
And then the next name. And then the next,
Soldiers of misfortune, lock-step into a star-colored tight dissolve,
History's hand-me-ons. But you, Father Candescence,
You, Father Fire?
                    Whatever rises comes together, they say. They say.

There Is a Balm in Gilead

Crows in a caterwaul on the limb-laced edge of the afternoon,
Three scored like black notes in the bare oak across the street.
The past is a thousand-mile view I can't quite see the end of.
Heart-halved, I stare out the window to ease its medicine in.

-•-

Landscape's a local affliction that has no beginning and no end,
Here when we come and here when we go.
Like white clouds, our poems drift over it,
                              looking for somewhere to lie low.
They neither hinder nor help.

-•-

Night sky black water,
                       reservoir crow-black and sky-black,
Starless and Godless.
Cars trundle like glowworms across the bridge, angel-eyed,
Silver-gilled.
          The fish in the waters of heaven gleam like knives.

-•-

I write, as I said before, to untie myself, to stand clear,
To extricate an absence,
the ultimate hush of language,
                         (fricative, verb, and phoneme),
The silence that turns the silence off.

-•-

Butt-end of January, leaf-ash and unclaimed snow,
Cold blue of blue jay cutting down to the feeder box,
The morning lit with regret,
No trace of our coming, no trace of our going back.

WILLIAM WRIGHT

Michelle in Rain

IN LOVE OF G. M. HOPKINS

I watch from window-dark light dim
        down and dwindle, fleck her haunted hair
                with leaves-sieved-rain, hymn
        for ear, eye, the moon cloud-caught, snared
though its gray ghost ghosts her limbs
        enough to see full form of her, her body flare
                under oak-arbor, whims
        of weighed-down, stone-stopped air.

        Streetlights strike and mist to find
her stare the lightning down, to still
        despite the ways these weathers twine, kill—
despite flash, flicker, mud-runnels-branch and thunder, signs
        that heaven's harrows haunt, may malign—
till this beauty summer's storm screams in, chilled.

A Path through Walnut Trees after Rain

To be clothed in the smell,
a skin of sweet-rot, flowery,
life-dark as a pond floor—
their fruit felled, wet, fat,
half-black, half-green in slack grass
sugared in bees and calyx sap,
where blue squill and fern lift
to a bedraggled sun
from this pocked ground,
its mosses bright, this vanishing,
and later, starblown night.

Aubade for Yellow Jacket

Dawn light sets them smoldering,
tiny gold-black fires that scorch the yard's
heart. They pulse: in, out, in, out

of a mud-ringed tear, where their crazed
focus seeks wood-pulp for nested tiers.
Guards click, seethe for queen and brood.

Something hums under this hill,
an open mouth that sucks the searing
sugars every June drips. Something

chews earth to paper dust and builds
these buried cells well into day's end,
when most dusks fail to douse

summer-stubborn heat. Grass crackles:
such a drone, a throb of anger here.
Hard to hate them for this madness

to outdo what will do them in, as fall
bleeds queens to flakes and new kin
hatch, winter-hidden, waiting.

Afterword

෨

G erard Manley Hopkins's influence on English poetry since the publication in 1918 of his poems by his friend and fellow poet, Robert Bridges, has been nothing short of extraordinary. Thinking of the many poets who have responded to his work, one would have to name T. S. Eliot, Wallace Stevens, Hart Crane, David Jones, W. H. Auden, Dylan Thomas, Elizabeth Bishop, Robert Lowell, John Berryman, Theodore Roethke, Sylvia Plath, Ted Hughes, William Everson (Brother Antoninus), Charles Wright, and Seamus Heaney. His influence also extends beyond the English-speaking world, his work having been translated into French, German, Spanish, Polish, Italian, Czech, Russian, Chinese, and Japanese. Every poet who has been influenced by Hopkins has, of necessity, focused on one or more aspects of Hopkins's work, fascinated, inspired, and often challenged by his word-chiming, complex epithets, or the way he mimics the action or what he called "the doing-be" of a particular thing, whether that be the wimpled wing of a kestrel or a stone falling into a roundy well, or the interiority of dizzying darkness likened to hanging from a cliffside in a storm.

There are so many aspects to Hopkins's poetry, each of them drawn by the logocentricity of his understanding of reality, which is that, as with the Big Bang theory of things, all creation came into Being in an instant of time—not in tick-tock time, but rather in kairotic time, in a flash, full—and moves out through the eons, only to return, finally, to its mysterious source, not as debris but as an imploding mosaic reassembled piece by piece into one: the Word made flesh made Word.

In mythic terms, that is what is at the heart of Hopkins's understanding of the Word and the plenitude of words, diamond dust, if you will, ignited by the fire that breaks forth from the Creator. And—synesthetically—by the sounds, the music Hopkins heard in the Welsh language, drawn as he was by its dappled *cynghanedd*, its word chiming, the play on the stops of consonants and vowels, lovely and yet strange, as if we were in a country where music was spoken, and which our hearts understood instantly, without translation, so that we found ourselves drawn to it as well.

Mix that with Hopkins's deep knowledge of the heroic-age Greek of Homer and Pindar, with their compound epithets running two and three deep—"dapple-dawn-drawn falcon," for instance, where the bird is drawn to the dappled dawn, as the Son to the Father, the soul to its Creator, and—in the action of that—the created thing drawn, etched out, transfigured by the dappled dawn. Add to that Hopkins's intense interest in the etymology of things, of their origins, of the first words multiplying and colonizing, as, for instance, in Hopkins's attempt to understand—via the etymology of things—how the names for the Greek gods came into being via the Egyptian gods who predated them by a millennia or more.

Or consider his long lists of words, their DNA spinning out from an earlier source, colonizing, stabilizing into their own distinctive identities here and here, no two words alike, each containing its distinctive nuances, "all things counter, original, spare, strange." Consider too Hopkins's interest in music, not in the late Nineteenth Century pianola lyrics in four-four time, or even the great symphonies of Beethoven and Bach, but something

older, much older: a music underlying the Greek choral sounds in Aeschylus and Eurip-
ides, or the soul calling out to its God in the Psalms at Qumran, or in the Benedictine
choirs at Monte Cassino, and which one hears in Hopkins's "Spelt from Sybil's Leaves,"
a poem which employs not only Welsh chiming, but something akin to chant and the
ancient Greek choruses.

This. And so much more.

No wonder we are so fascinated by Hopkins's poetry and why it remains so new, a
language with the dearest freshness deep down within it, a language like the waters at St.
Winifred's Well in his beloved Wales, with its ancient rivulets—like grace—flowing and
flowing again,

> steady as a water in a well, to a poise, to a pane,
> But roped with, always, all the way down from the tall
> Fells or flanks of the voel, a vein
> Of the gospel proffer, a pressure, a principle, Christ's gift.

As poets, each of us takes from Hopkins what he or she can, and admires it, imitates
it, or, because we are each distinctive, we drink from it, absorb it, and then apply the
distillation to creations of our own. Not to copy—as William Carlos Williams says—
but rather to imitate, which, according to Williams, is not an act of impersonation but
rather the chief work of the imagination. Of course, if you attempt to imitate Hopkins's
rich Welsh music you will have to ask yourself why, as a native of Massachusetts, say, or
Tennessee, you are doing so. Williams, for example, as much as he admired what Dylan
Thomas had wrought with the language, realized that he was going to have to avoid such
rich chiming in his own work because it belonged to another world, and certainly not the
language of New Jersey. And yet Wallace Stevens could be struck by the rich interplay of
sounds and colors in a line from one of Hopkins's sonnets, "the thunder-purple seabeach
plumèd purple-of-thunder." Rather like Stevens's own "dark / Encroachment of that old
catastrophe," or that "insolid billowing of the solid," or the "bird's fire-fangled feathers"
dangling down. Or later, in "An Ordinary Evening in New Haven," where New Haven
keeps playing in counterpoint against Hopkins's "heaven-haven."

Or consider Robert Lowell, in his "Quaker Graveyard in Nantucket," his Catholic
convert C.O. lament for his beloved country, written during World War II, as he watched
the US on its irretrievable way of transforming itself, as Rome had, from a republic into a
world empire. This is Milton's *Lycidas* rewritten as Hopkins's "Wreck of the *Deutschland*,"
only to be rewritten seventy years on by Lowell as he meshed the Bible, Milton, Melville,
and Hopkins into his own heartbreaking ode. For the young Lowell, that is, before he
turned from the Jesuit poet to court the skunk-scented flowers of Baudelaire, Hopkins
was much more than a poet. He was a figure, a model, to be emulated for his life as much
as for his words.

Or consider, too, John Berryman, shifting by degrees from his allegiance to Yeats
("I didn't want to be like Yeats," the young poet once said. "I wanted to BE Yeats") to
Hopkins. At Christmas 1966, Berryman was living in Dublin when he visited Hopkins's
unmarked gravesite where he lay with his Jesuit brothers in Glasnevin Cemetery. "Father
Hopkins, teaching elementary Greek," Berryman eulogizes,

whilst his mind climbed the clouds, also died here.
O faith in all he lost.
Swift wandered mad through his rooms & could not speak.
A milkman sane died, the one one, I fear.
His name was gone almost.

"A milkman sane died, the one one, I fear" paints Hopkins as the one really sane poet, drinking in milk from the heavenly Milky Way, gazing at those distant stars winking, which housed all the saints. Unlike Jonathan Swift, who went mad and lies buried now in Dublin. Unlike, perhaps—suicidal, depressed Henry feared—himself.

And, as this rich garland of poems which Daniel Westover and William Wright have gathered amply demonstrates, Hopkins still has the ability to evoke responses from a plethora of gifted poets. Charles Wright speaks for many of us when he writes, "For those who would rise to meet their work," the work of their own hands, Hopkins's work will serve as scaffolding, the poet as progenitor, the poet as "Father Candescence" and "Father Fire." And, like scaffolding, the more attuned we become to the fire that continues to break from Hopkins's poems, the more we turn to what Hopkins has to offer on so many levels, the more our own work might also rise, if I read Hopkins and Wright aright.

"I caught this morning morning's minion, king- / dom of daylight's dauphin," Hopkins sang back in May 1877 at the theologate at St. Beuno's in North Wales. How many of us have grasped for something of that energy, whether it be Morri Creech's egret striking its wings

> on the black water out near Pimlico,
> scanning for those widening, dimpled rings
> where fish break water.

or Libby Bernardin's great white pelicans, lifting "themselves with such / grace," as if some blessing had fallen upon her as she watched, lifting as from some white shawl, such as St. Peter envisioned the plenitude of creation there in Jaffa, "the black-tipped wings gathering air, / pulling themselves away from earth."

Or Jane Hicks's voice singing out, recalling a hawk somewhere over East Tennessee, brought back to life again, thanks to her nameless, blessed second-grade teacher's reading of Hopkins to her class:

> A hawk on thermals glided, soared, swooped among the kites,
> winged away, climbed high to wheel and hover, all below transfixed

and urging them on to "Ride the words like a hawk rides the wind," so that in time the poet would ride words that

> galloped on springs, swept off, soared again,
> fell into now, cloaked in *vermillion*,
> newest in my heart-cache of words.

Or to take another example from a plenitude of nature's possibilities, where even William Wright's angry, humming yellow jackets deserve our prayerful attention, as they pulse with diastolic life, as "Dawn light sets them smoldering, / tiny gold-black fires that scorch the yard's / heart." Or Katharine Whitcomb echoing Hopkins's "womb-of-all, home-of-all, hearse-of-all night" with her own "Blue of swoons, blue bruise, great inkdark, fogdark bank of night."

But I write this so that you may turn back to the poems themselves. Read them. Taste their beauty. Then read them again and again, measuring them against the world around you, as it shines through the words and the words in turn reveal afresh the world about you, a gift for the asking. And a word of deep thanks for the editors, who have brought together a stunning collection of poems, ranging from the bright neophyte to the seasoned, amber-rich voice, all of them part of a vibrant quilt of language, ringing in the air like the giant wind chime these poems play.

Paul Mariani

Contributors

ဢ

WIN BASSETT teaches and coaches at a boys' school in Nashville. His essays and interviews have been published by *The Atlantic, Oxford American, The Paris Review Daily, The Poetry Foundation*, and *The Washington Post*. His poems have appeared in *The Southern Poetry Anthology, Image, Ruminate*, and *Still: The Journal*. Win serves on the editorial staff of the *Virginia Quarterly Review*.

LIBBY BERNARDIN has two chapbooks, *Layers of Song* (Finishing Line Press, 2011) and *The Book of Myth* (Stepping Stones Press, 2009), which was one of six winners in the South Carolina Poetry Initiative chapbook contest. Her poems have appeared in numerous journals, including *Southern Poetry Review, The South Carolina Poetry Society Yearbook, Cairn, and Kakalak*. Her poems also appear in *The Southern Poetry Anthology, Volume I: South Carolina* and *After Shocks: The Poetry of Recovery for Life-Shattering Events*. Other publications over several years have included *Notre Dame Review, The Devil's Millhopper*, and *Negative Capability*.

ALLEN BRADEN is the author of *A Wreath of Down and Drops of Blood* (University of Georgia) and *Elegy in the Passive Voice* (University of Alaska/Fairbanks). His poems have been anthologized in *The Bedford Introduction to Literature, Poetry: An Introduction, Best New Poets* and *Spreading the Word: Editors on Poetry*. He lives in Lakewood, Washington.

STEVEN COLLIER BROWN is a poet and photography critic from southwest Louisiana. In 2010, he collaborated with photographer Jerry Uelsmann on a limited edition chapbook-length collection of poems and photographs called *Moth and Bonelight* (21st Editions). In 2013, he collaborated with photographer Ben Nixon on another book called *To the Wheatlight of June* (21st Editions). Brown is currently a PhD candidate in Harvard's American Studies program where he writes on nineteenth century aesthetics of waste in American literature and history. His poems can be found in *Best New Poets, Barrow Street*, and *Asheville Poetry Review*.

ROBIN CHAPMAN is the author of nine books of poetry, including *Abundance* (Cider Press Review), *the eelgrass meadow* (Tebot Bach) and *One Hundred White Pelicans* (Tebot Bach), poems of our changing terrain. A professor emerita of Communicative Disorders at the University of Wisconsin-Madison, she is a Fellow of the Wisconsin Academy of Sciences, Arts, and Letters.

MORRI CREECH was born in Moncks Corner, South Carolina in 1970 and was educated at Winthrop University and McNeese State University. He is the author of three collections of poetry, *Paper Cathedrals* (Kent State UP 2001), *Field Knowledge* (Waywiser, 2006), which received the Anthony Hecht Poetry prize and was nominated for both the Los Angeles Times Book Award and the Poet's Prize, and *The Sleep of Reason* (Waywiser, 2013), which was a finalist for the 2014 Pulitzer Prize. A recipient of NEA and Ruth Lilly

Fellowships, as well as grants from the North Carolina and Louisiana Arts councils, he is Writer in Residence at Queens University of Charlotte, where he teaches courses in both the undergraduate creative writing program and in the low residency MFA program. He lives in Charlotte, North Carolina with his wife and two children.

CAROLYN CREEDON's debut collection, *Wet* (2012), was chosen for the Stan and Tom Wick Poetry Prize by Edward Hirsch. Her work has also been featured in the anthologies *Best New Poets* (2009, edited by Kim Addonizio), *You Drive Me Crazy: Love Poems for Real Life* (2005, edited by Mary D. Esselman and Elizabeth Ash Vélez), and *The Best of the Best American Poetry: 1988–1997* (1998, edited by Harold Bloom). She earned a BA from Smith College, where she won the Glascock Prize, an MA from Washington University, and an MFA from the University of Virginia, where she won the Academy of American Poets Prize. Creedon has also won the Alehouse Happy Hour Poetry Prize, and her work was translated into Portuguese by Carlos Felipe Moises and published in the anthology *Alta Traição* (Unimarco Press, 2005). She lives in Charlottesville, Virginia.

PHILIP DACEY's latest of thirteen books of poems is *Church of the Adagio* (Rain Mountain Press, 2014), and his previous book, *Gimme Five*, won the 2012 Blue Light Press Book Award. Work of his appears in Scribner's *Best American Poetry 2014*. The winner of three Pushcart Prizes, Dacey is the author of complete volumes of poems about Gerard Manley Hopkins, Thomas Eakins, and New York City. After an eight-year post-retirement adventure as a resident of Manhattan's Upper West Side, he moved in 2012 to the Lake District of Minneapolis.

MEG DAY is 2015–2016 recipient of the Amy Lowell Poetry Travelling Scholarship, a 2013 recipient of an NEA Fellowship in Poetry, and the author of *Last Psalm at Sea Level* (Barrow Street, 2014), winner of the Barrow Street Press Poetry Prize and The Publishing Triangle's Audre Lorde Award, and a finalist for the 2016 Kate Tufts Discovery Award from Claremont Graduate University. Day is Assistant Professor of English and Creative Writing at Franklin and Marshall College and lives in Lancaster, Pennsylvania. Her website is www.megday.com.

R. H. W. DILLARD is the author of seven volumes of poetry (most recently, *What Is Owed the Dead*), with an eighth (*Not Ideas*) forthcoming, two verse translations of classical drama, two novels, a collection of short fiction, and two critical monographs. He is a Professor of English at the Jackson Center for Creative Writing at Hollins University, where he chaired the undergraduate and graduate creative writing program for thirty-two years. He lives in Roanoke, Virginia, where he manages a small but teeming wildlife habitat.

LYNN DOMINA is the author of two collections of poetry, *Corporal Works* (Four Way Books) and *Framed in Silence* (Main Street Rag), and the editor of a collection of essays, *Poets on the Psalms* (Trinity University Press). Her recent work appears or is forthcoming in *The Southern Review*, *The Gettysburg Review*, *The Massachusetts Review*, *Arts & Letters*, and several other periodicals. She currently lives in the western Catskill region of New York.

GEORGIA EDWARDS lives and writes in Georgia. "Come to Me" is her first publication.

DESMOND EGAN has published 23 Collections of Poetry, including *Selected Poems* (Creighton University Press, 1992), as well as two collections of essays, *The Death of Metaphor* (Colin Smythe, 1990) and *The Bronze Horseman* (The Goldsmith Press, 2009). He has also published translations of two Greek plays, *Medea* and *Philoctetes*. His poem "PEACE" was adopted as part of the "Peace for the Millennium" celebration and was translated into 35 languages. Egan has won numerous awards, including the Macedonian Poetry Prize, the Bologna Literary Award, The Farrell Prize, The Chicago Haymarket Literary Award and the National Poetry Foundation Award. In 2015, he was awarded the Chicago IBAM award for literature. Egan founded the Gerard Manley Hopkins Society's Gerard Manley Hopkins Festival in 1987 and has been its Artistic Director ever since. Born in Athlone, County Westmeath, Ireland, Egan is a full-time writer, living and working near Newbridge in County Kildare, Ireland.

JOHN FREEMAN lives in Harvey, Louisiana, where he is a retired teacher. His poetry has appeared in *Arkansas Review, Hawaii Pacific Review, The MacGuffin, Roanoke Review,* and *Xavier Review,* among other journals. He has published three books of poetry, the most recent *In the Place of Singing* (Louisiana Literature Press, 2005). He taught English and creative writing at Tarleton State University and Mississippi State University.

ALICE FRIMAN's sixth full-length collection is *The View from Saturn* (LSU Press). Her fifth collection is *Vinculum (*LSU Press), for which she won the 2012 Georgia Author of the Year Award in Poetry. She is a recipient of a 2012 Pushcart Prize and is included in *Best American Poetry 2009.* Friman lives in Milledgeville, Georgia, where she is Poet-in-Residence at Georgia College. Her podcast series, *Ask Alice,* is sponsored by the Georgia College MFA program and can be seen on YouTube.

TAYLOR GRAHAM is a volunteer search-and-rescue dog handler in the Sierra Nevada. She also helps her husband, Hatch (a retired wildlife biologist/forester) with his bird conservation projects. She's included in the anthologies *Villanelles* (Everyman's Library) and *California Poetry: From the Gold Rush to the Present* (Santa Clara University). Her latest book is *What the Wind Says* (Lummox Press, 2013), poems about living and working with her canine search partners over the past 40 years.

JESSE GRAVES is the author of two poetry collections, *Tennessee Landscape with Blighted Pine* (Texas Review Press, 2011), which won the 2012 Weatherford Award in Poetry from Berea College and the Appalachian Studies Association and the Book of the Year Award in Poetry from the Appalachian Writers' Association, and *Basin Ghosts* (Texas Review Press, 2014), which won the 2014 Weatherford Award in Poetry and for which he was recently awarded the 2014 Philip H. Freund prize from Cornell University. He has a PhD in English from the University of Tennessee and an MFA in Poetry from Cornell University. He teaches poetry writing and American literature at East Tennessee State University.

EVE GRUBIN's book of poems, *Morning Prayer*, was published by the Sheep Meadow Press. Her poems have appeared or are forthcoming in many American and UK literary publications, including *The American Poetry Review, The New Republic, PN Review, Poetry Review*, and *Conjunctions*, where her chapbook-size group of poems was featured and introduced by Fanny Howe. Her essays have appeared in various magazines and anthologies, including *The Veil: Women Writers on Its History Lore and Politics* (University of California Press, 2009) and *Jean Valentine: This-World Company* (University of Michigan Press 2012). Eve was the programs director at the Poetry Society of America and taught poetry at The New School University and in the Graduate Creative Writing Program at the City College of New York before she moved to London, where she now teaches at New York University in London. She is a tutor at the Poetry School and the poet in residence at the London School of Jewish Studies.

LUKE HANKINS is the author of *Weak Devotions* (Wipf & Stock, 2011) and the editor of *Poems of Devotion: An Anthology of Recent Poets* (Wipf & Stock, 2012). In 2014 he founded Orison Books, where he serves as editor. He also serves as Senior Editor of *Asheville Poetry Review*. Luke attended the Indiana University MFA program, where he held the Yusef Komunyakaa Fellowship in Poetry. His poems, essays, and translations have appeared in *American Literary Review, Contemporary Poetry Review, Image, New England Review, The Other Journal, Poetry East*, and *The Writer's Chronicle*, as well as on the American Public Media national radio program "On Being."

MARYANNE HANNAN's poems have appeared in *Christianity and Literature, Christian Century, The Other Journal, Gargoyle, Magma, 1110, Pebble Lake Review, Stand, Poet Lore*, and numerous anthologies. Formerly a Latin teacher, she lives in upstate New York. Her website is www.mhannan.com.

JEFF HARDIN, originally from Savannah, Tennessee, is an eighth generation descendant of the founder of Hardin County. He holds degrees from Austin Peay State University and the University of Alabama. A professor of English at Columbia State Community College in Columbia, Tennessee, he is the author of two chapbooks and four collections: *Fall Sanctuary*, recipient of the 2004 Nicholas Roerich Prize, *Notes for a Praise Book, Restoring the Narrative*, and *Small Revolution*. His poems have appeared in *The Southern Review, Hudson Review, Gettysburg Review, North American Review, Southwest Review, The New Republic, Poetry Northwest, Measure, Tar River Poetry, Meridian, Poet Lore*, and many others. His work has also been featured on *Verse Daily, Poetry Daily*, and Garrison Keillor's *The Writer's Almanac*.

DAVID HAVIRD is Professor of English at Centenary College of Louisiana. His poems have appeared in *Agni, Poetry, Sewanee Review, Yale Review*, and elsewhere. He has also published articles on such southern authors such as James Dickey, Flannery O'Connor, and Elizabeth Spencer in *Mississippi Quarterly, Southern Literary Journal*, and *Virginia Quarterly Review*. His collection of poems, *Map Home*, was published by Texas Review Press in 2013.

AVA LEAVELL HAYMON served as Poet Laureate of Louisiana from 2013–2015. Her most recent collection is *Eldest Daughter*, published by Louisiana State University Press. She has written three previous collections, *Why the House Is Made of Gingerbread*, *Kitchen Heat*, and *The Strict Economy of Fire*, all also from LSU Press, and edits the Barataria Poetry Series. Her poems have appeared in journals nationwide. Prizes include the *Louisiana Literature* Prize for poetry in 2003, the L. E. Phillabaum Poetry Award for 2010, and the Mississippi Institute of Arts and Letters 2011 Award in Poetry. *Why the House Is Made of Gingerbread* was chosen as one of the top ten poetry books of 2010 by Women's Voices for Change. A committed teacher of poetry writing, Ava worked as Artist in the Schools for a number of years, teaches poetry writing during the school year in Louisiana and, during the summer, directs a retreat center for writers and artists.

JANE HICKS, a native of upper East Tennessee, is an award-winning poet and quilter. Her poetry appears in both journals and numerous anthologies. Her first book, *Blood and Bone Remember*, was nominated for and won several awards, including Poetry Book of the Year from the Appalachian Writers Association. Her latest collection is *Driving with the Dead* (University Press of Kentucky, 2014). Jane's "literary quilts" illustrate the works of playwright Jo Carson and novelists Sharyn McCrumb and Silas House. The art quilts have toured with these respective authors and were the subject of a feature in *Blue Ridge Country Magazine* in an issue devoted to arts in the region.

JAN D. HODGE's poems have appeared in *New Orleans Review, North American Review, Iambs & Trochees, Defined Providence, South Coast Poetry Journal, Off the Coast, Lavender Review*, the *American Arts Quarterly* website, and many other print and online journals, in *Western Wind* (5th ed.), and in his chapbook *Poems to be Traded for Baklava*. His essay "Taking Shape: The Art of *Carmina Figurata*" appeared in *An Exaltation of Forms*, and *Taking Shape*, his collection of *carmina figurata*, was published in 2015 by Able Muse Press.

THOMAS ALAN HOLMES, a member of the East Tennessee State University English faculty, lives and writes in Johnson City. Some of his work has appeared in *Louisiana Literature, Valparaiso Poetry Review, The Connecticut Review, Appalachian Heritage, The North American Review*, and *The Southern Poetry Anthology*'s "Contemporary Appalachia" and "Tennessee" volumes. He is co-editor with Jesse Graves and Ernest Lee of *Jeff Daniel Marion: Poet on the Holston* (University of Tennessee Press).

JAY HOPLER is the author of two books of poetry, *Green Squall* and *The Abridged History of Rainfall*, and the editor (with Kimberly Johnson) of *Before the Door of God: An Anthology of Devotional Poetry* (Yale University Press, 2013). The recipient of numerous awards and honors, including the Yale Younger Poets Prize, a Whiting Award, and the Rome Prize in Literature, he teaches in the University of South Florida's writing program.

RON HOUCHIN has published work in *The James Dickey Review, The Hampden-Sydney Poetry Review, Still: The Journal*, and *Drafthorse*. A collection of short stories, *Tales Out of School*, was published by Wind Publications in 2012, and a new and selected poetry collection, *The Quiet Jars*, was released by Salmon Publishing of Ireland in 2013. Houchin's most recent collection is *The Man Who Saws Us in Half* (2013), part of Louisiana State University Press's Southern Messenger Poetry Series.

JOAN HOULIHAN is the author of four books of poetry: *Ay* (Tupelo Press, 2014); *The Us* (Tupelo Press, 2009); *The Mending Worm*, winner of the 2005 Green Rose Award from New Issues Press; and *Hand-Held Executions: Poems & Essays*. She has served as editor or reviewer most recently at *Contemporary Poetry Review*, and her critical essays are archived online at *bostoncomment.com*. Houlihan's work is anthologized in *The Iowa Anthology of New American Poetries* (University of Iowa Press) and *The Book of Irish-American Poetry* (University of Notre Dame Press). She is founder and director of the Colrain Poetry Manuscript Conference and serves on the faculty of Lesley University's Low-Residency MFA program.

JAMES CLINTON HOWELL holds an MA in English with an emphasis in poetry from the University of Southern Mississippi. His interests center on poetry, medieval history, and literary translation, particularly old and modern Germanic languages. His poems have been published in *The Southern Poetry Anthology Volume II: Mississippi, Flycatcher*, and elsewhere. He has also localized Japanese video games for American audiences and has written extensively for video game publications. He is a writer for Camouflaj Studio's acclaimed game *République*.

REBECCA GAYLE HOWELL is the author of *Render / An Apocalypse* (CSU, 2013), which was selected by Nick Flynn for the Cleveland State University First Book Prize and was a 2014 finalist for *ForeWord Review*'s Book of the Year. She is also the translator of Amal al-Jubouri's *Hagar Before the Occupation/Hagar After the Occupation* (Alice James Books, 2011), which was named a 2011 Best Book of Poetry by *Library Journal* and shortlisted for Three Percent's 2012 Best Translated Book Award. Among her awards are fellowships from the Fine Arts Work Center in Provincetown and the Carson McCullers Center, as well as a 2014 Pushcart Prize. Native to Kentucky, Howell is the Poetry Editor at *Oxford American*.

KIMBERLY JOHNSON is a poet, translator, and literary critic. Her collections of poetry include *Leviathan with a Hook*, *A Metaphorical God*, and *Uncommon Prayer*. Her monograph on the poetic developments of post-Reformation poetry was published in 2014. In 2009, Penguin Classics published her translation of Virgil's *Georgics*. Her poetry, translations, and scholarly essays have appeared widely in publications including *The New Yorker*, *Slate*, *The Iowa Review*, *Milton Quarterly*, and *Modern Philology*. Recipient of grants and fellowships from the John Simon Guggenheim Memorial Foundation, the National Endowment for the Arts, the Utah Arts Council, and the Mellon Foundation, Johnson holds an MA from the Johns Hopkins Writing Seminars, an MFA from the Iowa Writers' Workshop, and a PhD in Renaissance Literature from the University of California at Berkeley. She lives in Salt Lake City, Utah.

JOHN LANE is the author of a dozen books of poetry and prose. His latest, *Abandoned Quarry: New and Selected Poems*, was recently released by Mercer University Press. The book includes much of Lane's published poetry over the past 30 years, plus a selection of new poems. In 2012 *Abandoned Quarry* won the SIBA (Southeastern Independent Booksellers Alliance) Poetry Book of the Year prize. His latest prose books are *My Paddle to the Sea*, published 2011 by The University of Georgia Press, and *Begin with Rock, End with Water*, from Mercer University Press. He teaches environmental studies at Wofford College.

KEAGAN LEJEUNE lives in Lake Charles, Louisiana, where he teaches English and folklore at McNeese State University. Most recently his poems have appeared in *Louisiana Literature, The Southern Poetry Anthology*, and *Gilded Circles and Sure Trouble: The Art of Josephine Sacabo and Keagan LeJeune* (21st Editions).

GWYNETH LEWIS was the National Poet of Wales from 2005–2006, the first writer to be given the Welsh laureateship. She has published eight books of poetry in Welsh, her first language, and in English. Her most recent book of poems is *Sparrow Tree* (Bloodaxe, 2011). *Chaotic Angels* (Bloodaxe, 2005) brings together the poems from her three English collections, *Parables & Faxes, Zero Gravity and Keeping Mum*. She has also written two memoirs, *Sunbathing in the Rain* (Flamingo, 2002) and *Two in a Boat* (Harper Perennial, 2007). She was a television documentary producer and director at BBC Wales before leaving the BBC to become a freelance writer. Gwyneth is a Fellow of the Welsh Academy, a Fellow of the Royal Society of Literature and a NESTA Awardee (the National Endowment for Science, Technology and the Arts).

ED MADDEN teaches at the University of South Carolina, and he serves as Poet Laureate for the City of Columbia, SC. He is the author of a previous chapbook and three previous books of poetry, including *Signals*, winner of the South Carolina Poetry Book Prize, and his most recent collection, *Ark*. His poems have appeared in a wide range of journals, as well as in *Best New Poets 2007* and *The Book of Irish American Poetry*. He has also published his work on Irish literature and culture in *Eire/Ireland*, the *Canadian Journal of Irish Studies*, and the *Irish University Review*.

MAURICE MANNING Maurice Manning's most recent books are *The Gone and the Going Away* and *The Rag-Picker's Guide to Poetry*, co-edited with Eleanor Wilner. His fourth book, *The Common Man*, was a finalist for the Pulitzer Prize. A former Guggenheim fellow, Manning teaches at Transylvania University and in the MFA Program for Writers at Warren Wilson College.

AMIT MAJMUDAR is a diagnostic nuclear radiologist who lives in Columbus, Ohio, with his wife and three children. In 2015, he was named as Ohio's first Poet Laureate. His work has appeared or is forthcoming in *The New Yorker, The Atlantic Monthly, The Best American Poetry* anthology, *The Best of the Best American Poetry 1988–2012, The New York Review of Books, The New Republic, Poetry Magazine, Poetry Daily* and other venues, including the 11th edition of the *Norton Introduction to Literature*. His first novel,

Partitions, was published by Holt/Metropolitan to wide acclaim, with featured reviews in *The Wall Street Journal* and NPR's *All Things Considered*. His first poetry collection, *0*, *0*, was released by Northwestern in 2009. His second poetry collection, *Heaven and Earth*, was awarded the Donald Justice Prize for 2011. His most recent novel, *The Abundance*, was published by Picador in 2014. His newest collection of poetry is *Dothead* (Knopf, 2016). His website is www.amitmajmudar.com.

SANDRA MARCHETTI is the author of *Confluence*, a debut full-length collection of poetry from Sundress Publications (2015). She is also the author of four chapbooks of poetry and lyric essays, including *Sight Lines* (Speaking of Marvels Press, 2016), *Heart Radicals* (ELJ Publications, 2016), *A Detail in the Landscape* (Eating Dog Press, 2014), and *The Canopy* (MWC Press, 2012). Sandra's poetry appears widely in *Subtropics, Ecotone, Green Mountains Review, Word Riot, Blackbird, Southwest Review*, and elsewhere. Her essays can be found at *The Rumpus, Words Without Borders, Mid-American Review* and other venues.

PAUL MARIANI is the University Professor of English at Boston College, specializing in Modern American and British Poetry, religion and literature, and creative writing (memoir, biography, and poetry). He has published nearly 300 essays, introductions, chapters in anthologies and scholarly encyclopedias, and reviews, as well as being the author of 18 books. These include biographies of William Carlos Williams, John Berryman, Robert Lowell, Hart Crane, Gerard Manley Hopkins, and—most recently—Wallace Stevens. His biography of Williams was a Finalist for the National Book Award. He has published seven volumes of poetry, most recently *Epitaphs for the Journey*, as well as commentaries on Hopkins, Williams, and many others. He is also the author of *Thirty Days: On Retreat with the Exercises of St. Ignatius*. His awards include a Guggenheim Fellowship and several National Endowment for the Arts and National Endowment for the Humanities Fellowships. He has taught poetry workshops at the Bread Loaf Writers Conference and the Glen Workshops, and in 2009 he received the John Ciardi Award for Lifetime Achievement in Poetry. His life of Hart Crane, *The Broken Tower*, a feature-length film, directed by and starring James Franco, was released in 2012. He is now at work on a memoir of growing up on the mean streets of New York in the 1940s and an eighth volume of poetry, *Ordinary Time*.

CHRISTOPHER MARTIN is the author of the poetry chapbook *A Conference of Birds* (New Native Press 2012) Some of Martin's poems and essays have appeared or are forthcoming in *Shambhala Sun, Ruminate Magazine, Thrush Poetry Journal, Drafthorse, Still: The Journal, Buddhist Poetry Review, Adventum, Poecology, The Museum of Americana: A Literary Review, Loose Change Magazine, Revolution House, Pale Ale Press*, American Public Media's *On Being* blog, and elsewhere. His poems "Revelation on the Cherokee County Line" and "Antidote to Narcissus" were selected to appear in the *Southern Poetry Anthology, Volume V: Georgia*. His poem "Marcescence," published as a broadside by Thrush Press in October 2012, was nominated for a Pushcart Prize. Martin is the founder and editor-in-chief of the online literary magazine *Flycatcher* and is a contributing editor at *New Southerner*, where he writes the monthly blog *Kairos and Crisis* on race, religion, and social justice in the South.

MARIANA MCDONALD's poetry has appeared in *Fables of the Eco-Future*, *The Southern Poetry Anthology: Georgia*, *Sugar Mule*, *The Southern Women's Review*, *From a Bend in the River: 100 New Orleans Poets*, and *El Boletín Nacional*. She became a Fellow of Georgia's Hambidge Arts Center in 2012. A bicultural poet writing in English and in Spanish, Mariana lives in Atlanta, where she is active in the poetry community and in social justice movements. She works as a public health scientist.

ASHLEY ANNA MCHUGH's debut poetry collection, *Into These Knots*, was the 2010 winner of The New Criterion Poetry Prize. She was the 2009 winner of the Morton Marr Poetry Prize, and her poems have appeared in *Nimrod*, *The Journal*, *Smartish Pace*, and *Measure*, as well as in other publications.

LUCIEN DARJEUN MEADOWS's poetry has appeared in *West Branch*, *Hayden's Ferry Review*, *Quarterly West*, and the *American Journal of Nursing*. An AWP Intro Journals Project winner, he has been nominated for the Pushcart Prize and received recognition from the Academy of American Poets. Lucien lives in Fort Collins, Colorado.

PHILIP METRES is the author of a number of books and chapbooks, most recently *Pictures at an Exhibition* (2016), *Sand Opera* (2015), and *abu ghraib arias* (2011). His work has appeared in *The Best American Poetry*, and *Inclined to Speak: Contemporary Arab American Poetry*, and has garnered two NEA fellowships, the Thomas J. Watson Fellowship, four Ohio Arts Council Grants, the Beatrice Hawley Award, the Anne Halley Prize, the Arab American Book Award, and the Cleveland Arts Prize. He teaches at John Carroll University in Cleveland, Ohio.

SUSAN LAUGHTER MEYERS is the author of *My Dear, Dear Stagger Grass* (2013), winner of the Cider Press Review Editors' Prize. Her collection *Keep and Give Away* (University of South Carolina Press, 2006) received the South Carolina Poetry Book Prize. Her work has also been published in numerous journals and anthologies, including *The Southern Review*, *Prairie Schooner*, and *Crazyhorse*. A long-time writing instructor, she has an MFA from Queens University of Charlotte. She lives in the rural community of Givhans, South Carolina, with her husband Blue.

MAREN O. MITCHELL's poems have appeared in *Iodine Poetry Journal*, *The Lake* (UK), *Appalachian Heritage*, *The South Carolina Review*, *Hotel Amerika*, *Southern Humanities Review*, *Skive* (AU), *The Classical Outlook*, *Town Creek Poetry*, *The Journal of Kentucky Studies*, *Appalachian Journal*, anthologies *Negative Capability Press Anthology of Georgia Poetry*, *The Southern Poetry Anthologies, V: Georgia* and *VII: North Carolina*, *Sunrise from Blue Thunder*, and elsewhere. Work is forthcoming in *Hotel Amerika*, *Chiron Review*, and *Poetry East*. Her nonfiction book is *Beat Chronic Pain, An Insider's Guide* (Line of Sight Press, 2012). She lives with her husband in the mountains of Georgia.

MEREDITH MOENCH was born in Scotland to American ex-patriot parents and split her growing up years between Scotland and Germany before moving to Illinois, where she won several literary awards at Wheaton College. Her poetry has appeared in

Kodon, Pub, and elsewhere. She now lives in Kosovo, where she works in art therapy among women at risk.

ROBERT MORGAN is the author of fifteen books of poetry, most recently *Dark Energy* (2015). He has also published nine volumes of fiction, including *Gap Creek,* a *New York Times* bestseller. A sequel to *Gap Creek, The Road from Gap Creek,* was published in 2013. His new novel, *Chasing the North Star,* was published in April 2016. Robert is the author of three nonfiction books, *Good Measure: Essays, Interviews, and Notes on Poetry; Boone: A Biography;* and *Lions of the West: Heroes and Villains of the Westward Expansion.* He has been awarded the James G. Hanes Poetry Prize by the Fellowship of Southern Writers, and the Academy Award in Literature by the American Academy of Arts and Letters. Recipient of fellowships from the Guggenheim and Rockefeller foundations, the National Endowment for the Arts, and the New York State Arts Council, he has served as visiting writer at Davidson College, Furman, Duke, Appalachian State, and East Carolina universities. A member of the Fellowship of Southern Writers, he was inducted into the North Carolina Literary Hall of Fame in 2010. Since 1971 he has taught at Cornell University, where he is Kappa Alpha Professor of English.

ANGELA ALAIMO O'DONNELL is a writer, poet, and professor at Fordham University in New York City where she teaches English, Creative Writing, and American Catholic Studies. She is the author of six books of poems, most recently *Lovers' Almanac* (2015), *Waking My Mother* (2013) and *Saint Sinatra & Other Poems* (2011), and three books of prose, including a memoir, *Mortal Blessings,* and a biography, *Flannery O'Connor: Fiction Fired by Faith* (2015). Angela's poems have appeared in many journals, including *America, Christian Century, Comstock Poetry Review, Concho River Review, First Things, Hawaii Pacific Review, Mezzo Cammin.com, New Texas, Pedestal Magazine.com, Post Road, Potomac Review, Relief, RUNES: A Review of Poetry, String Poetry, The Nepotist.org, Valparaiso Poetry Review, Verse Wisconsin, Vineyards, Windhover, and Xavier Review.* She has been nominated for Pushcart and Best of the Web prizes and was a finalist for the Foley Poetry Award, the Elixir First Book Award, and the Mulberry Poets & Writers Award.

MELISSA RANGE's first book of poems, *Horse and Rider* (Texas Tech University Press, 2010), won the 2010 Walt McDonald Prize in Poetry. Range is the recipient of awards and fellowships from the National Endowment for the Arts, the Rona Jaffe Foundation, the American Antiquarian Society, and the Fine Arts Work Center in Provincetown. Recent poems have appeared in *32 Poems, Ecotone, Image, New England Review, Subtropics,* and other journals. Her second book, *Scriptorium,* is a 2015 National Poetry Series winner and is forthcoming from Beacon Press. Originally from East Tennessee, she currently lives in Wisconsin, where she is an assistant professor of English at Lawrence University.

RON RASH is the Parris Distinguished Professor in Appalachian Cultural Studies at Western Carolina University. In 1994 he published his first book, a collection of short stories titled *The Night the New Jesus Fell to Earth.* Since then, Rash has published five collections of poetry, six short story collections, and six novels, most recently *Above the*

Waterfall (Ecco, 2015). Rash's poems and stories have appeared in more than one hundred magazines and journals. Ecco released his *New and Selected Poems* in March.

JANEEN PERGRIN RASTALL lives in Gordon, MI, population 2. She is the author of the chapbook, *In The Yellowed House (dancing girl press, 2014).* Her poetry is forthcoming or has appeared in several publications including: *North Dakota Quarterly, The Fourth River, Border Crossing, Dunes Review,* and *Raleigh Review.* She has been nominated for two Pushcart Prizes.

JOSHUA ROBBINS is the author of *Praise Nothing* (University of Arkansas Press, 2013). His recognitions include the James Wright Poetry Award, the New South Prize, selection for the *Best New Poets* anthology, and a Walter E. Dakin Fellowship in poetry from the Sewanee Writers' Conference. He is Assistant Professor of English and Creative Writing at University of the Incarnate Word. He lives in San Antonio.

DON SHARE is the editor of *Poetry* magazine. His most recent books are *Wishbone* (Black Sparrow, 2012), *Union* (Eyewear, 2013), and *Bunting's Persia* (Flood Editions, 2012); he has also edited a critical edition of Bunting's poems for Faber and Faber (forthcoming). His translations of Miguel Hernández, awarded the *Times Literary Supplement* Translation Prize and Premio Valle Inclán, were published in a revised and expanded edition by New York Review of Books (2013), and also appear in an edition from Bloodaxe Books (1997). His other books include *Seneca in English* (Penguin Classics, 1998), *Squandermania* (Salt, 2007), and *The Open Door: 100 Poems, 100 Years of POETRY Magazine* (University of Chicago Press, 2012), co-edited with Christian Wiman. His work at *Poetry* has been recognized with three National Magazine Awards for editorial excellence from the American Society of Magazine Editors, and he received a VIDA Award in 2015 for his "contributions to American literature and literary community."

DEREK SHEFFIELD's book of poems, *Through the Second Skin* (Orchises, 2013), was the runner-up for the 2012 Emily Dickinson First Book Award and a finalist for the Washington State Book Award. His work has also appeared in *Poetry, The Georgia Review, The Southern Review,* and *Orion.* He has received fellowships from Artist Trust and the Sustainable Arts Foundation. He teaches poetry and nature writing at Wenatchee Valley College where he also works as an advocate for sustainability and environmental humanities. He lives with his family in the foothills of the Cascades near Leavenworth, Washington, and serves as the poetry editor of *Terrain.org.*

MARK SMITH-SOTO has been editor or associate editor of *International Poetry Review* at the University of North Carolina at Greensboro for over twenty years. Along with four prize-winning chapbooks he has authored three full-length poetry collections, *Our Lives Are Rivers* (University Press of Florida, 2003), *Any Second Now* (Main Street Rag, 2006) and *Time Pieces* (Main Street Rag, 2015). His work, which has appeared in *Antioch Review, Kenyon Review, Literary Review, Nimrod, Rattle, The Sun* and many other publications, has been nominated several times for a Pushcart Prize and was recognized in 2006 with an NEA Fellowship in Creative Writing.

CHERYL STILES has published numerous poems, essays, and reviews in journals such as *Poet Lore, 32 Poems, The Atlanta Review, storySouth, Slant, Plainsongs, Southern Women's Review*, and *Poem*. Her work has received the Agnes Scott Literary Festival Prize and a Pushcart nomination. As a member of the Georgia Writers Registry, she gives readings and workshops throughout the southeast. She works as a university librarian in Atlanta and is completing a doctoral degree at Georgia State University.

MARY SZYBIST is the author of *Granted*, a finalist for the National Book Critics Circle Award, and *Incarnadine*, winner of the 2013 National Book Award for Poetry. She is the recipient of fellowships from the Guggenheim Foundation, the National Endowment for the Arts, the Witter Bynner Foundation in conjunction with the Library of Congress, the MacDowell Colony, the Rockefeller Foundation's Bellagio Center, and two Pushcart Prizes. She teaches at Lewis & Clark College in Portland, Oregon.

R. K. R. THORNTON is co-editor of *The Collected Works of Gerard Manley Hopkins, Vols. 1 and 2* (Oxford University Press, 2013). Prior to retiring in 2000, Kelsey was Professor of English and Head of Department at the University of Birmingham. He previously held the same position at the University of Newcastle upon Tyne. He has written on and edited the poetry of Hopkins, John Clare, the Decadents, Ivor Gurney, Nicholas Hilliard, Ernest Dowson, F. W. Harvey, and W. W. Gibson, and he has edited the Journals of the John Clare Society (1990–96) and the Ivor Gurney Society (from 1995 until the present). His book *Adlestrophes* (Rectory Press, 2014), explores how other poets would have approached the material of Edward Thomas's famous poem, re-writing the poem as if in their voices.

PIMONE TRIPLETT is the author of three book-length collections of poetry, *Rumor* (Triquarterly/Northwestern, 2009), *The Price of Light* (Four Way Books, 2005), and *Ruining the Picture* (Triquarterly/Northwestern, 1998). A winner of the Larry Levis Poetry Prise and the Oregon Book Award, she is also co-editor of *Poet's Work, Poet's Play* (University of Michigan, 2008), a collection of essays on poetic craft. She teaches at the University of Washington MFA Program in Seattle.

DAMIAN WALFORD DAVIES, a poet, librettist and academic, has published four collections of poetry between 2006 and 2015: *Whiteout, Suit of Lights, Witch*, and *Judas*. He has just completed *Docklands*, a ghost story in verse set in the dock area of Cardiff in the 1890s. He has published widely on British Romanticism and the two literatures of Wales. Chair of Literature Wales and a Fellow of the Welsh Academy, Damian is Professor of English Literature and Head of the School of English, Communication and Philosophy at Cardiff University.

DANIEL WESTOVER is a poet and literary critic. His poems have appeared in *North American Review, Crab Orchard Review, Tar River Poetry, Southeast Review, Spoon River Poetry Review, Measure, Asheville Poetry Review*, and in several recent anthologies, including *The Southern Poetry Anthology: Tennessee* and *Poems of Devotion: An Anthology of Recent Poets*. He is the author of *R. S. Thomas: A Stylistic Biography* (University of Wales Press, 2011), a critical biography of the Welsh priest-poet. Forthcoming books include *Michael Fargo's*

Epistle (a novel) and *Leslie Norris: a Ghost Story* (a biography). Daniel holds an MFA from McNeese State University and a PhD from the University of Wales. He is currently Associate Professor of English and Director of Graduate Studies at East Tennessee State University.

KATHARINE WHITCOMB is the author of four collections of poems: *The Daughter's Almanac* (The Backwaters Press, chosen by Patricia Smith as the winner of the 2014 Backwaters Prize), *Lamp of Letters* (Floating Bridge Press, winner of the 2009 Floating Bridge Chapbook Award), *Saints of South Dakota & Other Poems* (Bluestem Press, chosen by Lucia Perillo as the winner of the 2000 Bluestem Award), and *Hosannas* (Parallel Press, 1999). She teaches at Central Washington University and lives in Ellensburg, Washington.

SARAH ANN WINN's poems, flash fiction, and hybrid works have appeared or will soon appear in *Five Points, Massachusetts Review,* and *Passages North,* among others. Her chapbooks include *Field Guide to Alma Avenue* and *Frew Drive* (forthcoming, Essay Press, 2016), *Haunting the Last House on Holland Island* (forthcoming, Porkbelly Press, 2016), and *Portage* (Sundress Publications, 2015). Visit her at bluebirdwords.com or follow her @blueaisling.

JOHN WOOD received the 2009 Gold Deutscher Fotobuchpreis for *Endurance and Suffering: Narratives of Disease in the 19th Century,* published by the German press Edition Galerie Vevais. He is the only poet to win the Iowa Poetry Prize twice, first for *In Primary Light* (1993) and second for *The Gates of the Elect Kingdom* (1996). His *Selected Poems 1968–1998* was published by University of Arkansas Press in 1999, and his latest collection, *The Fictions of History,* was published by 21st Editions in 2012. Wood is also a leading art and photography critic whose books have won many awards. He co-curated the 1995 Smithsonian Institution/American Art Museum exhibition "Secrets of the Dark Chamber." He is Professor Emeritus of English literature and photographic history at McNeese State University in Lake Charles, Louisiana, where he directed the Master of Fine Arts Program in Creative Writing for over twenty-five years. He and his wife Carol now live in Saxtons River, Vermont.

WILLIAM KELLEY WOOLFITT holds a BA from Fairmont State University, an MA from Hollins University, and an MFA and PhD from Pennsylvania State University. Woolfitt teaches creative writing and literature at Lee University. He has worked as a summer camp counselor, bookseller, ballpark peanuts vendor, and teacher of computer literacy to senior citizens. He is the author of *The Salvager's Arts,* co-winner of the 2011 Keystone Chapbook Prize. His writings have appeared or are forthcoming in *Threepenny Review, Cincinnati Review, Michigan Quarterly Review, Ninth Letter, Shenandoah,* and other journals. His full-length book, *Beauty Strip,* won the Southern Poetry Breakthrough Prize for Tennessee (Texas Review Press, 2015).

CHARLES WRIGHT, Poet Laureate of the United States, was born in Pickwick Dam, Tennessee, in 1935 and was educated at Davidson College and the University of Iowa. His books include *Sestets: Poems* (Farrar, Straus and Giroux, 2010); *Littlefoot: A Poem* (2008); *Scar Tissue* (2007), which was the international winner for the Griffin

Poetry Prize; *Buffalo Yoga* (Farrar, Straus & Giroux, 2004); *Negative Blue* (2000); *Appalachia* (1998); *Black Zodiac* (1997), which won the Pulitzer Prize and the Los Angeles Times Book Prize, *Chickamauga* (1995), which won the 1996 Lenore Marshall Poetry Prize; *The World of the Ten Thousand Things: Poems 1980–1990*; *Zone Journals* (1988); *Country Music: Selected Early Poems* (1983), which won the National Book Award; *Hard Freight* (1973), which was nominated for the National Book Award, among others. He has also written two volumes of criticism and has translated the work of Dino Campana in *Orphic Songs* as well as Eugenio Montale's *The Storms and Other Poems,* which was awarded the PEN Translation Prize. He is Souder Family Professor of English at the University of Virginia in Charlottesville.

WILLIAM WRIGHT is author four full-length book of poetry, including *Tree Heresies* (Mercer University Press, 2015), *Night Field Anecdote* (Louisiana Literature Press, 2011), *Bledsoe* (Texas Review Press, 2011), and *Dark Orchard* (Texas Review Press, 2005), as well as four chapbooks, including *Sleep Paralysis,* which won the South Carolina Poetry Initiative Prize (chosen by Kwame Dawes). Wright is series editor and volume co-editor of *The Southern Poetry Anthology,* a multivolume series celebrating contemporary writing of the American South, published by Texas Review Press. Additionally Wright serves as assistant editor for *Shenandoah* and is co-editor (with Daniel Cross Turner) of *Hard Lines: Rough South Poetry* (forthcoming from the University of South Carolina Press).

Printed and bound by CPI Group (UK) Ltd, Croydon, CR0 4YY

13/04/2025

14656573-0005